Home Runs

Home Runs

Tales of Tonks, Taters, Contests and Derbies

Andy Strasberg

**August
Publications**

Contents

Home Runs: Tales of Tonks, Taters, Contests and Derbies

August Publications
5115 Excelsior Blvd.
#734
St. Louis Park, MN 55416
augustpublications.com

Cover by Natalie Nowytski.

Printed in the United States of America.

Library of Congress Control Number: 2022950373

ISBN 978-1-938532-75-7 (Print)
ISBN 978-1-938532-76-4 (eBook)

9 8 7 6 5 4 3 2 1

For my wife Patti and our puppy Pippa.

Foreword: Duane Kuiper

Growing up, my team was the Milwaukee Braves with home run hitters Hank Aaron, Eddie Mathews, Wes Covington and Joe Adcock. Aaron was my favorite. And while there's no denying the home run was a big part of my 12-year big-league career—as we see in the game today—only one homer stands out for me.

It came on August 29, 1977. I was with the Cleveland Indians in my third big-league season. We were playing the White Sox in Cleveland's Municipal Stadium. The game was televised regionally for ABC's *Monday Night Baseball*, which meant a large TV audience nationwide, but blacked out in the greater Cleveland area.

At that point of the season, we were 61-69 and 17 games out of first place, in fifth place. Since the All-Star Game, we were red-hot, hitting .280 plus, while scoring 29 runs in our last three games and winning 15 of 21.

I was swinging the bat pretty good with a respectable .281 batting average. On that day I was hitting second in the lineup.

Steve Stone (13-10) a tough right-hander, was on the mound for the South Siders.

Even though this was our home ballpark, there was a banner parading around proclaiming, "South Euclid Loves Steve Stone." Seeing that banner kind of defeats the home-field advantage, but hopefully they were paying customers.

As the game got underway, to get things started, my chance was in the first inning after Paul Dade struck out.

I took a couple of practice swings. Stepped into the batter's box. Looked out at Stone.

The first pitch was a ball. Then Stone threw me a fastball. I hit it high...I hit it deep...and I hit it...outta there!

The ball landed in the second, maybe the third row of the right-field stands occupied by no more than ten fans, maybe 11 that I counted as I headed to second base.

Fortunately, my homer hit an empty seat and bounced back towards the field. The rebound was caught by White Sox right fielder Wayne Nordhagen, who threw it in to our dugout so I could add it to my collection.

After I rounded third, I gave myself one big clap, then slapped the outstretched right palm of our third-base coach, Joe Nossek.

As I crossed home plate, our next batter, Buddy Bell, was there with his right hand extended for another congratulatory palm slap. One more time, I clapped my hands together. As I approached the dugout, I shook hands with our bat boy and was greeted by the entire Indian bench.

What a thrill. My first home run.

Immediately, I knew that with 31 games left in the season if I hit 1.96774194 homers every game, I could pass Roger Maris and the single-season home run record would be mine.

Just as I had intended, my home run started the momentum because following my blast, Andre Thornton and Bruce Bochte connected to make it three round-trippers in just the first inning against Stone.

Later, in the sixth inning, I knocked in a run with a single and started a key double play, making a diving grab behind second base on a hard-hit grounder from Don Kessinger.

We won that game 9-2 in front of 6,236 hometown fans, including those turncoat fans with the Steve Stone banner.

After the game, Bob Sudyk of the *Cleveland Press* asked me what my thoughts were as I rounded the bases.

I responded, "Actually, I didn't think of anything. When I got back to the dugout, I tried to think back: Did I touch all the bases?"

The next day, the *Akron Beacon Journal* plastered my name as top billing in the headlines as our team was on a homer binge.

Another paper's headline took it further, "Henry Aaron can move over: here comes big Duane Kuiper."

One story led with the line, "Power hitting Duane Kuiper walloped a first inning homer."

I was quoted in the papers: "It was exciting, believe me. At first, I didn't think it was going out."

It was without question the biggest home run of my career. Still is.

But enough about me and my home run hitting prowess.

In the following pages of *Home Runs: Contests, Derbies, Tales & Tonks*, you will find home run information that has either long ago been forgotten or been buried for decades.

Among many treats, you will read about Babe Ruth's side business of barnstorming that almost always included a home run, along with the misleading grand-slam homer record held by Lou Gehrig.

There's also a great collection of behind-the-scenes stories about the San Diego Padres' pre-game home run derbies featuring Willie Stargell, Terry Kennedy, Dave Kingman and Hank Aaron.

My personal behind-the-scenes Aaron story is about a ball that he hit that one-hopped the fence, which is probably why it wasn't included in this book. It should have been.

It happened in March 1975 during spring training.

I couldn't believe my good fortune that as a kid idolizing Aaron, here I was playing second base for the Indians and Aaron was the DH for the Brewers at Hi Corbett Field in Tucson, Arizona.

In the first inning Hank hit a double off Jim Kern that one-bounced the fence at the 405-feet sign.

As the next batter stepped into the batter's box, Henry took a small lead off second base, then a pick-off play was called. Aaron was so startled that he spiked himself going back to the bag to avoid the tag.

Instantly, he gave me a glance that I interpreted as, what are you doing? I think I mouthed, "Not me," while gesturing toward our manager, Frank Robinson, who was in the dugout looking at Hank with a broad grin.

But I digress.

Visually, you will be treated to recently unearthed photos taken at a 1961 North Carolina home-run exhibition that had been mislabeled and largely forgotten until Andy Strasberg brought them to light.

I'm sure baseball history lovers will enjoy Andy's conversation with long-time baseball author, Arnold Hano, an eyewitness to home runs from Babe Ruth to Barry Bonds.

After all these years, I realize how fortunate I was to have played in the big leagues and how blessed I am to broadcast games for the San Francisco Giants.

Fortunately, I had the pleasure of calling many of Barry Bonds' homers. He made my job as a broadcaster easy because he didn't just hit fly balls to the warning track: "He hit 'em high, he hit 'em deep…he hit 'em **outta here!**"

If you love the long ball, *Home Runs: Contests, Derbies, Tales &*
Tonks touches 'em all.

Duane Kuiper is a long-time commentator and play-by-play
announcer for the San Francisco Giants. The 1977 home run Duane
Kuiper describes was hit in his 1,382nd career at-bat, the only home
run he hit in a 12-year big-league career encompassing 3,754 plate
appearances.

Chapter 1

Leading Off

Baseball players who didn't work on farms or enjoyed permanent jobs in the early 1900s searched for opportunities to earn money during the offseason. This was a practicality: They knew that close to a couple hundred days would come and go before they'd be able to earn a salary as a ballplayer once again.

As a result of their baseball-playing abilities and the game's growing popularity, supplementing those baseball salaries between one season to the next led to the era of barnstorming—that is, playing a series of exhibition games in non-MLB cities—a tradition almost as old as the game.

By all accounts, baseball's first barnstorming tour involved the 1860 Brooklyn Excelsiors, who would play other teams for an agreed-on fee. Over the next decade, it became common practice for the game's best players, if not entire teams, to band together for offseason barnstorming tours, usually held on a regional basis. (Yes, the practice of *barnstorming* is older than the term *barnstorming*, which has its roots in post-WWI pilots traveling from barn to barn in rural areas for exhibitions.)

The 1860 Brooklyn Excelsiors were also known as the Jolly Young Bachelor Base Ball Club.

By 1910, to protect their investment in players and the potential of injuries, baseball's team owners banded together to add this following contractual clause regarding such exhibitions:

"The party of the second part (the player) will not be permitted at any time, either during the playing season or before the commencement or after the close thereof, to participate in any exhibition baseball games, indoor baseball, basketball, or football, except that the consent of the party of the first part (the club) has first been secured in writing."

The owners didn't withhold permission for players to earn a few extra bucks, but they wanted to be "in the know," and, to a degree, control the players' outside baseball activities.

Then the game experienced perhaps the most significant

impact since players began wearing gloves instead of fielding bare-handed, when the home run arrived on the scene in 1919.

Not "Home Run" Baker kind of home runs—who, according to baseball lore, earned his nickname by hitting only two homers to win Game 2 and Game 3 of the 1911 World Series against the Giants—but the Babe Ruth "Sultan of Swat" kind of home-run numbers, when he hit 29 in 1919, then 54 in 1920 and 59 in 1921.

George "Babe" Ruth, c. 1920. Courtesy Library of Congress, LC-USZ62-71763.

As the popularity of barnstorming increased, so did the contractual restrictions of players.

Consider Section 8B of Article 4 of the Major League code, which took effect in February 1921: "Both teams that contest in the world's series are required to disband immediately after its close and the members thereof are forbidden to participate as individuals or as a team in exhibition games during the year in which that world's championship was decided."

Following the 1921 Fall Classic, baseball commissioner Judge Kenesaw Mountain Landis fined New York Yankees teammates Babe Ruth, outfielder Bob Meusel and right-handed pitcher Bill Piercy, suspending all three until May 20 of the 1922 season.

Led by Ruth, the offending Yankees had taken part in a series of exhibition games without permission.

For owners and now the players, baseball was a big-time business with significant financial implications. In addition to wins and losses, the allure of home runs, how many were hit and by whom, became baseball's extra added attraction and drawing card.

Additionally, home-run contests would be a standalone form of entertainment, held before games on both amateur and professional levels, eventually becoming the central theme of the syndicated 1960s TV series, *Home Run Derby*.

Chapter 2

First Pitch

Thanks to Babe Ruth swatting an unthinkable amount of homers, those hit *after* the baseball season were also newsworthy.

This headline of October 17, 1920 edition of the *La Crosse Tribune* in La Crosse, Wisconsin says it all: "Ruth Knocks Home Run in Barnstorming Game."

The wire story pointed out that in Jersey City, New Jersey, "Ruth made one of his customary home runs, which have been usual features of the games played by his team on its barnstorming trip."

The term "Home Run Derby" was being used by newspapers almost on a daily basis during the regular season when describing either the home run leaders of a league or if multiple home runs were hit in a single game.

One such example occurred in the May 17, 1922 edition of the *Los Angeles Evening Express* newspaper. A cartoon graphically compared Kenneth Williams of the St. Louis Browns, who had 11 homers for the season, and the Yankees' Babe Ruth, who was still in the starting gate as a result of not having played a game due to the removal of his tonsils on May 4, 1922.

- According to the *Topeka State Journal,* Tillie Walker, left fielder for the Philadelphia Athletics, stepped up with the leaders in the home-run derby by hitting Numbers 26 and 27 during a doubleheader against the Cleveland Indians on August 15, 1922.
- Bob Meusel of the Yankees hit six homers in seven days to warrant the May 18, 1925 edition of the *Washington Post* to run this headline in the sports section: "Bob Meusel Climbs in Home Run Derby."
- The *Reading Times* printed a story about how baseball teams could attract additional fans, adding it was common for minor-league teams to stage a side attraction of players competing against each other before the regular game competing in a 100-yard dash, throwing for accuracy and throwing for distance.

But it was the home-run contest garnering the most expressions of *oohhs* and *aahhs.*

- In Reading, before the Keystones' game against the Buffalo Bisons at Lauer's Park on June 15, 1931, Bill Barrett won the distance contest by throwing a ball 370 feet and then copped the home-run contest to win a suit by Weiner's, a menswear store. George Quellich, who finished in second place, won a fountain pen.
- The June 9, 1933 ballgame at Philadelphia's Shibe Park between the Yanks and A's featured home runs from New York's Lou Gehrig and Tony Lazzeri, as well the Phillies' Jimmie Foxx. The next day a *Washington Post* headline proclaimed "Yankees Win in Battle of Home Runs," as New York won, 7-6.

- In the September 29, 1934 edition of the *News-Journal* of Mansfield, Ohio, it was noted that "one of the stunts on Sunday's bill at League Park is a home run hitting contest, letting the best sluggers of the Cleveland Indians and Chicago White Sox swing at 10 pitches each."

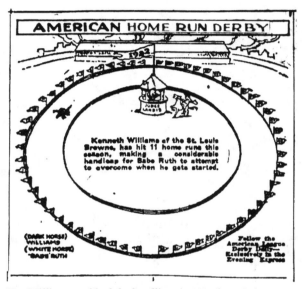

Ken Williams grabbed the headlines in 1922 from Babe Ruth.

Chapter 3

"The Show"

To the delight of sports fans, TV's embryonic beginnings in the early 1950s delivered a variety of sports programming into homes around the country. For those sports enthusiasts who didn't live close to sports venues or were unable to afford in-person tickets for major sports events—boxing matches, baseball, football and basketball games—TV was a welcome (and free) addition to their homes.

Against this backdrop came the syndicated, 30-minute series *Home Run Derby*, created in 1959 by three enterprising TV veterans:

- Jack Harvey, an experienced TV writer and producer of the 1950s, most notably for *The Ford Television Theater*
- Lou Breslow, an established Hollywood screenwriter and film director dating back to the late 1920s
- Mark Scott, an actor and play-by-play voice of the Pacific Coast League's Hollywood Stars

Home Run Derby's first show began with the two popular players competing against each other.

Here were the original contest rules:

1. Each week, two stars from the major leagues meet to determine who can hit the most home runs.

2. A fair ball hit over the fence is scored as a home run. A ball that remains inside the park is an out.

3. Batters need not swing at every pitch, but a strike (as called by home plate umpire) is an out.

4. Three outs per inning. Nine innings per game (unless tied).

5. The batter with the most home runs at the game's end wins $2,000 and an invitation to defend his title the following week. His opponent (the loser) gets $1,000 and is eliminated.

6. A player who hits three consecutive home runs in a single time at bat wins $500 bonus. Four straight in a time at-bat—$1,000. And for each consecutive home run after that, $1,000 more.

7. Pitchers do their best to "groove" the ball and serve up home-run balls, because they also receive a bonus for giving up the most home runs. Pitchers alternate each inning so that they get an equal opportunity to pitch to both batters.

The incentive for players to participate was a guarantee of $1,000 (plus expenses).

The incentive to win was $2,000 (plus expenses).

The Home Run Derby scoreboard was modestly simple but did the job.

THE BALLPARK

The *Home Run Derby* competition was filmed at Los Angeles's Wrigley Field beginning in late 1959, with the show entering syndication in 1960. Built in 1925 by Los Angeles Angels and Chicago Cubs owner William Wrigley Jr., it opened as the original Wrigley Field, as the Chicago version would not bear the moniker until November 1926. Home to the Pacific Coast League's Los Angeles Angels until 1957, the ballpark had been without professional baseball after the Brooklyn Dodgers moved to Los Angeles in early 1958, making it available for filming the series. It had been in use as a television/movie set over the years, however, with movies like *Damn Yankees* and TV shows like *The Munsters* filmed there. It also served as home of the expansion American League Los Angeles Angels for a single year, in 1961.

Other contributing factors included Southern California's usually mild climate in January and the ballpark's proximity to the Hollywood movie-making industry.

Plus, according to host Mark Scott, the fence distances were symmetrical, favoring neither American Leaguers or National Leaguers, although Scott probably meant right-handed or left-handed hitters.

Indeed, once the show aired, TV viewers could plainly see that the ballpark fences were not symmetrical. The dimensions of the former minor-league ballpark

The host of Home Run Derby, Mark Scott was corny, camp and clever.

were 340 feet down the left field line and 339 feet down the right field line. It was 412 to dead center, but just 345 feet in the power alleys.

The left-field wall was a few feet higher than the right-field wall, which had an inner fence with palm trees and a brick wall several feet behind.

For any ball hit in that direction to count as a home run, it had to clear the brick wall or hit the top of the trees that stuck out over the wall. This was done because the distance was shorter to right field with the inner fence, which would otherwise give a lefty an unfair advantage.

THE EXTRAS

The pitchers for the show were actually right-handed outfielders possessing strong and, it was hoped, accurate pitching arms:

- Tom Saffell, a former Hollywood Star and Los Angeles Angels outfielder in the minors, was with the Pittsburgh Pirates in 1949-51 and 1955 and the Kansas City Athletics in 1955; and
- Clarence Maddern, who came up with the Chicago Cubs in 1946 and played for Chicago in 1948 and 1949. He was also with the Cleveland Indians in 1951.

The pitchers alternated every other inning and were incentivized with an undisclosed amount of cash for whomever served up the most gopher balls.

The catchers were Eddie Malone, who had played for the Chicago White Sox in 1949 and 1950 and then spent several seasons with the Hollywood Stars, and John Van Ornum, who had just begun his minor-league baseball career in 1959.

Umpiring behind the plate was retired big-league ump Art Passarella. He would call pitches that were strikes but weren't swung at. There were two foul line umpires for the purpose of calling balls fair or foul that went over the fence.

THE PILOT

Once the show's producers agreed about how the competition would unfold, it was time to move the concept from paper to film.

The *Home Run Derby* pilot was shot in black-and-white film in Wrigley Field on November 24, 1959.

The players pitted against each other were the last two players to have hit 50 homers in a season: Mickey Mantle (52 homers in 1956) of the New York Yankees and Willie Mays (51 homers in 1955) of the San Francisco Giants.

Much like a heavyweight prize fight, the two sluggers went head-to-head, battling it out for nine innings.

The first contest could not have been better if it had been scripted. "The Mick" beat the "Say Hey Kid" by hitting a homer in the bottom of the ninth to break a tie, winning by a score of 9-8, "winning all the marbles," according to host Mark Scott.

Once the film was edited for TV, fans had a rare opportunity to watch players in closeup shots, hitting and responding to Scott's questions during the contest.

The show's pilot was a success.

The remaining 25 shows were again filmed at Wrigley Field, with shooting scheduled for three weeks in January 1960. Each episode, without commercials, was 24 minutes in duration and took approximately four hours to shoot.

SYNDICATION & SPONSORS

The February 20, 1960 trade publication *SPONSOR* included an article written by Len Firestone, the VP of Syndication, Ziv Television Programing, Inc., New York, which read in part:

A brand-new sports concept in television, Home Run Derby, high-lighting the most powerful batsmen in both leagues contending in a

World Championship home run competition for awards as high as $10,000 a "game," and reaching a total of $250,000 for the season.

Home Run Derby will inaugurate the first man-to-man all-star baseball competition in TV history, accenting the big men in the "big moment" of the national pastime. We expect its impact on the medium to be as formidable as the pioneering Sea Hunt.

Ziv Television Productions, the company that was founded by Frederick Ziv in 1948 and who was considered as the father of television first-run syndication, handled the syndication and distribution.

As reported in the August 22, 1960 issue of SPONSOR, the show appeared in 49 states and 159 markets, ranging from Alaska to New York to Santa Barbara to Florida in markets such as WALB, Albany, Georgia; WJAR, Providence; KLIX, Twin Falls, Idaho; KTVE, El Dorado, Arkansas; KDIX, Dickinson, North Dakota; WEAU, Eau Claire, Wisconsin; WTVT, Tampa, Florida; WBAL, Baltimore; and KDKA-TV, Pittsburgh.

In addition to securing nearly 30 automotive dealers in the national client list, other sponsors included Consolidated Cigar Company, International Harvester, and several breweries, including Milwaukee's Schlitz, Philadelphia's Esslinger and Canada's Labatt.

THE SLUGGERS

Participating contestants were from the National and American Leagues. Fifteen of the 16 major-league teams were represented, with the Chicago White Sox as the lone unrepresented team.

Perhaps the White Sox's absence was due to team members being busy with other business opportunities after winning the 1959 American League pennant. Or maybe it was because, offensively, the "Go-Go" Chicago White Sox were known for their speed, not long-ball prowess.

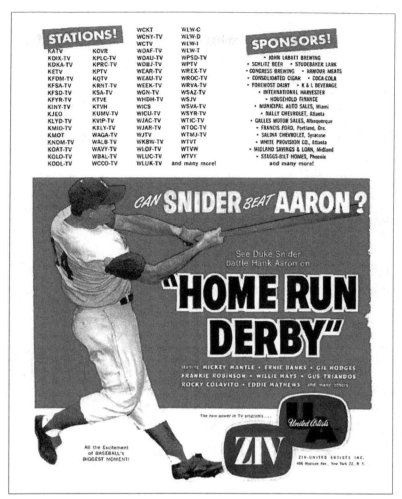

Same time same station next week.

In fact, they hit fewer homers than any other big-league team during the 1959 season, which meant that pickings were slim when it came to sluggers. Sherm Lollar led the team with 22 round-trippers and Al Smith came in second with 17.

In addition to Mays and Mantle, who competed in the first show, other popular stars featured were Hank Aaron, Eddie Mathews, Rocky Colavito, Ernie Banks, Gil Hodges, Duke

Snider, Jackie Jensen, Frank Robinson, Dick Stuart, Harmon Killebrew, Bob Allison, Wally Post, Gus Triandos, Bob Cerv, Ken Boyer, Al Kaline and Jim Lemon.

Only two of the show's sluggers hit left-handed: Duke Snider and Eddie Mathews.

Mantle, the lone switch-hitter, decided to bat from the right side against right-handed pitchers because during his career he had hit longer homers from that side of the plate.

PUBLICITY

As a result of notes published in the sports and entertainment sections of newspapers around the country, *Home Run Derby* enjoyed additional publicity in the hometowns of the participating players' teams during the dead of winter.

One such example: baseball-starved fans in Milwaukee were notified that the show would film Hank Aaron competing on January 4 and then Eddie Mathews on January 7, to be aired at a later date.

JACKIE JENSEN
BOSTON RED SOX

Jensen was the first man to play in the Rose Bowl, the World Series and the MLB All-Star Game.

PLAYER INTERVIEWS

The show's host was Mark Scott, whose real name was Samuel Marks Solomon. He was an actor and radio broadcaster whose background included play-by-play for the Pacific Coast League's Hollywood Stars and one season with the Cincinnati Reds in the mid-1950s.

In 1959, Scott, a close friend of Joe DiMaggio's, was also part of a potential investment group, including entertainer Dean Martin and actor Jack Webb, looking to own a franchise in Bill

Shea's nascent plan to create a third baseball major league, the Continental League.

The television show opened with Scott introducing the players competing against each other. He then explained the rules, adding a reminder at least once during the broadcast that, "It's a home run or nothing here on *Home Run Derby.*"

Situated not far from the batter's box in back of home plate was where Scott handled play-by-play while the sluggers took their cuts. Scott sat behind what appeared to be a metal office desk inside a tent.

On the desk was his score sheet, a copy of Hy Turkin's *Official Encyclopedia of Baseball* (to which he never referred when on-camera) and a desktop microphone, capturing his play-by-play, interspersed with chit-chat and questions to the batter's opponent seated to his left.

Here are samples of Scott's verbal tête-à-tête, which was part of the show's somewhat awkward charm:

Scott to Bob Cerv: "Bob, what weight bat do you generally swing?"

Scott to Rocky Colavito: "Rocky, are you much of a wrist hitter or more of an arm hitter?"

Scott to Jim Lemon: "Do you hit with your wrists?"

Scott to Gus Triandos: "Gus, you seem to be getting your swing a little bit better now."

Gus: "I hope you're right."

Mark: "You haven't hit any yet (pause). But you will."

NUMBERS

The most home runs hit in a single game was 25, when Jackie Jensen faced off against Ernie Banks, winning 14–11.

Jensen's 14 home runs against Banks were the most any player hit in a single contest.

The fewest round-trippers in a contest from both participants was four, when Hank Aaron competed against Duke Snider and won, 3-1.

Mickey Mantle hit the most home runs, a total of 44 during his five appearances.

Hank Aaron collected the most cash for his participation, $13,500.

Home Run Derby began hitting the airwaves on April 4, 1960, coinciding with the start of the major-league season.

GAME NOTES

Some of the *Home Run Derby* contests were squeakers, a couple were blowouts and a few were dramatic bottom-of-the-9th thrillers.

HUSH TONES: It would be Mays, who unknowingly triggered some campy humor after hitting two homers in a row. So as not to distract his concentration, Mays asked Mark Scott to remain quiet while he batted in the 7th inning of the game against Harmon Killebrew.

Scott handled it perfectly.

Rather than move the mic on the desk closer to himself, he leaned over to the mic and whispered as if Mays was on the 18th green trying to sink a 50-foot putt: "Two home runs in a row for Mays. He doesn't want me to talk about it too loud. Another home run for Willie here would be $500. $500 pitch coming up."

Mays connected but pulled it foul to break his consecutive home run string at two.

GET A GRIP: Killebrew was one of the few players to use pine tar on the handle of his bat for a better grip.

GUM IT UP: Although no official records were kept on the matter, it appeared that Harmon Killebrew and Dick Stuart led the sluggers in the unofficial gum-chewing competition.

IN-N-OUT: The first extra-inning contest was between

Harmon Killebrew and Rocky Colavito. Killer's one-out fly ball in the bottom of the 10th inning hit the top of the left field wall and bounced over to end the game.

THE WIS KIDS: Interestingly, the only two players to face each other from the same team were Eddie Mathews and Hank Aaron of the Milwaukee Braves. Hank beat Eddie in the bottom of the 9th with a homer that broke the three-all tie.

AND NOW A WORD FROM THE UMP: Eddie Mathews was the first left-handed batter on the show, which gave veteran ump Passarella the opportunity to cite the ground rules as they applied to balls hit to right field.

SWINGING IN THE RAIN: There were a couple of games played in the rain. The first was Gil Hodges vs. Ernie Banks. In the last half of the third inning, on a Hodges pop-up to the infield, Scott announced, "High pop-up. That can't bring rain," adding, "We already have some."

In another contest, obviously filmed the same day as the rain fell, Banks faced Jackie Jensen. In the bottom of the 5th inning, Jensen donned a rain jacket after his turn at-bat.

Scott, who recalled Mays' concern regarding his loud broadcast, said after Banks hit two home runs in a row, whispered quietly into the mic, "Another one here is a bonus of $500."

Banks hit it out. After his at-bat, he also put on a light raincoat.

UNIFORM CHANGES: For the filming, Rocky Colavito appeared in a #6 Cleveland uniform. But on April 17, two days prior to the start of the 1960 season, he was traded to the Detroit Tigers for Harvey Kuenn, whose uniform number was #7.

The trade was fodder for sportswriters and fans because "Rock the Sock" was the American League's home run champ of 1959 with 42 circuit clouts.

As for Kuenn, he was the American League's batting champ with .353, making this the only time in baseball history that a league's batting champion had been traded for a home run champion.

As an extra-added bonus, not only did the players trade uniforms, they also traded uniform numbers.

HBP: In the Harmon Killebrew vs. Ken Boyer contest, the pitcher was struggling to find the strike zone. In the bottom of the 2nd inning with Killebrew at the plate, the second pitch made him turn away as if it was a brush-back.

During Killebrew's next at-bat, as if the problem was the baseballs, home plate umpire Art Passarella asked to examine the ball, which seemed most peculiar taking into account that the baseballs were new.

A few pitches later, one of Killebrew's drives hit the left-field foul pole. The ball dropped to the top of the fence and bounced over for a homer. Killebrew also hit one down the line that provided the home plate ump an opportunity to yell, "Foul ball!"

In the top of the 9th, the pitcher's strike zone woes continued when Ken Boyer got plunked by a pitch.

GOOD LUCK AND GOOD-BYE: In the bottom of the 9th with Ken Boyer leading Harmon Killebrew, Boyer implied that he needed some luck to win, so he respectfully asked Scott, "You don't mind if I sit here with my fingers crossed, do you?"

TRAFFIC STOP: Other than the sound of the crack of the bat meeting the ball, the natural ambience sound was street traffic just outside the ballpark along 42nd Place.

HOME SWEET HOME: It didn't appear that there was any reason why some players wore home uniforms and others wore their away togs. With filming in only black and white and teams sporting the same design for home and away uniforms— remember, this was the pre-color-TV era—it was difficult to tell which uniforms were white or gray. Players wearing their home uniforms (Mantle, Colavito, Boyer, Hodges) were easily outnumbered by those wearing road uniforms.

GROUND RULE HOMER: Duke Snider hit a home run off

the right-field palm trees in the 6th inning of his contest against Hank Aaron.

SHADOW FACTOR: As the sun slowly set in the Southern California sky, the cameras caught the shadows cast by Wrigley Field across the darkening infield.

BUTTER HANDS: Since many of the players hadn't swung a bat since the conclusion of the previous season, their hands were susceptible to blisters, which explained the unusual appearance of players wearing golf gloves for protection.

BALLPARK BOUNCER: Many of the homers clearing the left-field wall could be seen bouncing higher than the wall after hitting 42nd Place.

IT'S IN THE CARDS: To promote the TV show, a set of 20 black-and-white (3 1/4" x 5 1/4") baseball cards of the sluggers was produced by American Motors, the show's sponsor.

The cards, which also included host Mark Scott, were handed out at the carmaker's dealerships across the country.

To highlight the beginning of *Home Run Derby* TV show, Yankees infielder Gil McDougald was on hand at a car dealership in West Hartford, Connecticut on April 25, 1960. He gave away autographed pictures of himself, plastic bloop baseballs and *Home Run Derby* baseball cards.

MAKE SOME NOISE: According to outfield shagger Jim Marshall, who saw playing time for the Baltimore Orioles and the Chicago Cubs in 1958, then exclusively for the Cubs in 1959, one of Aaron's homers made a clanging noise as the ball "landed smack dab in a big garbage can on the other side of the wall."

A BANK SHOT: In the last show after Jackie Jensen hit his fifth consecutive home run in a row, but missed number six, Mark Scott mentioned to his opponent Mickey Mantle that Jackie was still smiling.

Mickey quickly responded with his charismatic grin and

friendly Oklahoma accent, "I don't blame him for smiling. I'd be rolling on the ground laughing up there if I did it."

In the bottom of the fourth inning Mantle makes himself laugh with a comment to Mark Scott about Jackie Jensen's display of home run power.

NEWS CLIPS

It was reported that after he won a total of $6,000, Dick Stuart, who competed on January 18 in two contests, went out and purchased a $10,000 Cadillac.

Jackie Jensen, whose 1959 contract with the Red Sox, according to Associated Press reports, was between $32,500 to $35,000. For competing in the *Home Run Derby* he won $8,500.

Then, on January 25, 1960 he retired from baseball, citing his desire to be with his family and avoid traveling.

∾

The amount of money *Home Run Derby* pitchers earned was revealed to be $100 for every homer they served up, according to writer Terry Young in the March 6 edition of *The Monitor* newspaper of McAllen, Texas.

∾

In May of 1960, UPI's Fred Danzig wrote a review article about the TV show. It was basically a recap of how the contest worked. The only insight Danzig provided was that the photography was functional and that viewers wouldn't learn anything about the art of hitting a pitched ball.

He concluded his column with these prophetic words: "*Home Run Derby* is dedicated to the further glorification of the home run, money, and the home run hitter."

∾

Lou Breslow was quoted by writer Pete Kokon in the May 3, 1960 edition of the *North Hollywood Valley Times* that a total of "$84,000 was paid out for 290 homers."

∾

The show's director, Ben Stoloff, credited Killebrew with the longest poke. "Harmon picked on a cripple and sent it sky-high toward left-center field," Stoloff said. "If it hadn't hit right below the top of the light tower, it would have gone into orbit."

∾

Mark Scott was quoted in the *Mirror News* of Los Angeles that the shows cost Ziv $478,000 to make.

AFTERWORD

After the show, the producers offered each of the competing players a bonus of $500 for signing an option to do the show for the next four years.

~

Once the last show was "in the can," the editing process of the approximately four hours of film down to 24 minutes commenced.

~

Frank Scott (no relation to Mark Scott) represented most of the players on the TV show for product endorsements, speaking engagements and appearances. As a result of the show's first-season success, it would have been practical for him to envision a steady income stream for the players participating, as well as his commission.

Unfortunately, as a result of Mark Scott's sudden death from a heart attack at 45 years old in Burbank on July 13, 1960, the producers opted not to replace him and instead cancelled the show outright.

Chapter 4

"Boom"

As a result of the nationally syndicated 1960 TV show *Home Run Derby* the popularity of home run hitting contests continued to blossom during the 1961 baseball season.

Even big-league light-hitting batters were participating.

An example would be Boston center fielder Gary Geiger, who had been in the big leagues since 1958 and was not known for his home-run prowess. As of July 4 of the 1961 season Geiger had hit a total of 29 homers in his big-league career. Yet he won $100 in a pregame home-run contest when the Red Sox were in Washington, D.C., to play the Senators on July 4, 1961.

With the Yankees playing Washington in Griffith Stadium on July 18, the Senators scheduled their second annual "Roll Call Night" with a delegation of members of Congress, their families and friends numbering approximately 1,500 as guests.

Prior to the game, there was a home-run hitting contest with three players from each team partnered with an elected official, who each had an at-bat to hit homers.

Roger Maris was paired with thirty-five-year-old Republican Representative Charles E. Goodell of Jamestown, New York. (Goodell was the father of National Football League Commissioner Roger Goodell.) Maris managed to hit one homer off the five pitches he saw.

Roger Maris with Rep. Carroll D. Kearns (R-Pennsylvania) and Rep. Charles E. Goodell (R-New York).

Fifty-six-year-old Republican Representative Edwin Dooley of Mamaroneck, New York, was partnered with Mickey Mantle, who won the contest by hitting three of five pitches out of the park. One of Mantle's pregame shots hit the last row of the left-field bleachers.

According to newspaper reports, none of the lawmakers reached the fence.

During the contest, when Mantle was batting there came a steady booing from the Yankee bench. Turns out the boo-bird was Whitey Ford, who explained after the contest that he wanted Mick to feel at home, referring to the fact that Yankee Stadium fans boo Mantle every time he doesn't homer.

Mantle was awarded a $100 bond for winning and earned a season pass to the remaining Senators home games for his partner Dooley.

The Yanks won the game by a score of 5-3, putting the Yanks in first place as Mick hit two homers, which tied him with Maris at 35 each for the season.

~

The Detroit Tigers had Rocky Colavito and Norm Cash take their hacks against the Baltimore Orioles' Jim Gentile and Gus Triandos in a pregame contest on July 20 in Detroit.

Each player was given eight fair balls. Each player knocked three over the fence, so a playoff round took place in which each player was allowed three swings. Triandos connected twice and won the hundred bucks in prize money, Cash came in second place, while Gentile and Colavito tied for third place.

In 2021 Gentile recalled that contest, "Yes, I remember," he said decades later. "I came in dead last with Colavito. We had to split $75. That's $37.50 a piece. Triandos won it. Cash came in second. The night before I hit a two-run homer and we won the game by two runs. And the night I lost the home-run hitting contest before the game but in the game I hit two home runs. It didn't matter, as we lost 15 to 8."

~

As a fundraiser for the benefit for sandlot baseball in the New York metropolitan area Yankee management scheduled an exhibition game against the San Francisco Giants at Yankee Stadium on July 24, 1961.

This would be the first time the Giants played in New York since they left for San Francisco after the 1957 season.

The game was delayed for twenty-two minutes after rain muddied the field, which canceled batting practice and a home run contest featuring Willie Mays and Orlando Cepeda vs. Roger Maris and Mickey Mantle.

In the game Mick hit a home run in his first at-bat. That homer, according to the wire service, traveled 420 feet. Mays, who was the major draw, drove in the winning runs with a single. San Francisco won 4–1 in front of 47,346 fans.

Newspaper scribes around the country were showing off their creative writing skills by acknowledging the home run duel between Maris and Mantle with hopefully a catchy new name. In the August 21, 1961, edition of the *Daily News* sportswriter Joe Trimble has labeled the home run derby as the M&M "Beltathon."

Chapter 5

M&M Guessing Contests

By late August 1961 newspapers across the United States were flooded with guessing contests, featuring entry blanks for fans to win money if they could predict the number of homers Maris and Mantle would hit.

The *New York Daily News* ran weekly contests coupons for prize money totaling $1,500. Contest information was written by sportswriter Red Foley as if it was a story. He politely ended one of his write ups with, "Remember now, the coupon will be available tomorrow. Fill it out and send it in. Mantle 'n Maris will do the rest."

The *Pittsburgh Press* ran a Mantle-Maris Home Run Derby guessing contest with the winner receiving five hundred bucks. In addition to guessing the number of homers hit in both 154 games and 162 games, the paper has, for the purpose of avoiding a tie, included a few other guesses, such as how many RBI for each player.

∿

Other newspaper contests appeared in Abilene, Texas; Marshall, Texas; Passaic, New Jersey; Miami, Florida; San Francisco, California; Honolulu, Hawaii; Charlotte, North Carolina; Greenville, South Carolina; Sapulpa, Oklahoma; and Reno, Nevada. The interest in home runs was not confined to the United States.

The *London Sunday Observer* from England had a thousand-word story about the home-run race in their September 20, 1961 edition. The headline read: "Babe Ruth Legend Under Siege." Paul Gardner wrote the article as he tried to put the game of baseball in terms the English could understand. "In cricket terms," he pointed out, "a home run is roughly equivalent to a six hit in front of the wicket."

Newspapers across the United States held contests for fans to guess how many homers the Yankee Sluggers would hit. Prize money ranged from $12.50 to $1,500 or a new men's suit from Gray Reid's men's shop. Decision of the Judges is final.

Chapter 6

North Carolina '61 Gopher Derby

I n the late afternoon of October 9, a moment after Cincinnati's Vada Pinson check-swing pop fly was caught in Crosley Field's shallow left by Hector Lopez to end the 1961 World Series, Roger Maris was the first Yankee off the field and into the visitors clubhouse, where he quickly showered, dressed and hustled to catch a 5:50 p.m. flight home to Kansas City.

He left behind a disastrous .105 average, notching only two hits in nineteen at-bats for the Series—the worst productivity among position pitchers with more than one at-bat.

When Roger and his wife Pat arrived in Kansas City, they were greeted by a crowd of a hundred fans, including the president of the Raytown, Missouri Chamber of Commerce, Dr. Dillard Eubank, who presented Pat with a bouquet of yellow and white mums.

Unable to go directly home, they were escorted to Raytown City Hall in suburban Jackson County, where they received a key to the city in a short ceremony. A caravan of about twenty cars escorted by patrolmen from Raytown convoyed them to their home at 5120 Blue Ridge Boulevard.

After a physically exhausting and mentally challenging baseball season, Maris had six days before he would board a plane for North Carolina to participate in a five-city home run derby exhibition throughout the state.

~

Occasionally, but more often than you think, history repeats itself. Even in baseball.

Baseball's home-run leader in 1927 was Babe Ruth. His business manager during his playing career was Christy Walsh, who handled his extracurricular money-making opportunities, apart from his playing contract with the Yankees.

Walsh's business dealings ranged from movies, endorsements, merchandise and appearances to book deals and barnstorming tours.

Baseball's home run leader in 1961 was Roger Maris, whose business manager during his playing career, beginning in 1960, was Frank Scott, who handled his extracurricular money-making opportunities, other than his playing contract with the Yankees.

Scott's business dealings ranged from movies, endorsements, merchandise and appearances to book deals and barnstorming tours.

~

It was during the dog days of the 1961 baseball season when Scott became aware of interest in staging a home run derby exhibition in at least four North Carolina cities after the World Series.

Maris was physically and mentally exhausted after the 1961 season.

The idea was put forth by Matt Boykin, who ran a construction company before switching full-time to baseball in his mid-40s to become the owner and president of the Wilson Tobs

(Tobacconists) baseball club of the Class-B Carolina League. As a business, the Tobs struggled to turn a profit. Three years earlier, after the 1958 season, the Tobs were approximately $6,500 in debt.

Some reports indicated that Boykin tried each year to somehow make ends meet for the Tobs, a farm club of the Washington Senators and then the Minnesota Twins.

Boykin's 1961 manager was Jack McKeon, who upon reflecting recently on the tour, said "'61 was the year of the home run, and Matt wanted to do something special for the people of North Carolina."

The idea was to provide North Carolina baseball fans who couldn't get enough of the 1961 American League's home run race the opportunity to watch a homer hitting exhibition between three of the game's best sluggers.

New home run king Roger Maris was joined by two other junior-circuit sluggers, Harmon Killebrew of the Twins and Jim Gentile of the Orioles, both of whom would end the 1961 season with 46 homers.

The aforementioned Frank Scott, handling endorsements and personal appearances across the MLB world, took on the responsibility of recruiting the players for the Derby.

Gentile remembers his invitation: "It was the last month of the 1961 season. Frank Scott came into the Orioles clubhouse, introduced himself and asked me if I would be interested in going on a home run hitting tour down South with Killebrew and Maris.

"I said, Yeah, why not. He told me that I'd get a thousand dollars a day. I joked about it and thought, gee whiz, that's four grand. I don't have to work this winter for the Orioles making appearances."

Gentile was alluding to the Orioles' winter speakers bureau along with Jackie Brandt, Jack Fischer, Milt Pappas, Steve Barber and Gus Triandos.

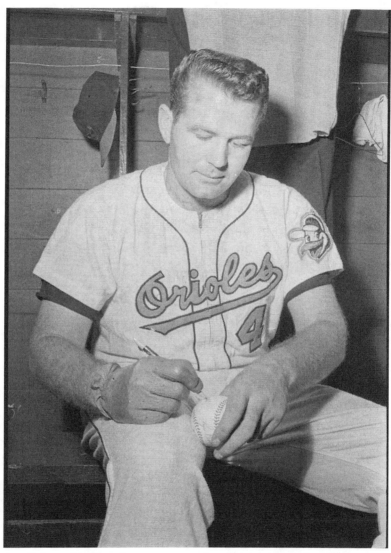

Gentile began his minor league career as a 2-6 pitcher in the Dodgers organization.

Diamond Jim further explained, "An organization would call in and ask for an Oriole to give out Little League trophies. It could be in Baltimore or out of town like York, Pennsylvania.

"We got paid $50 if the engagement was in Baltimore and $75 out-of-town, plus gas.

"I could have a noon luncheon in town talking to the Kiwanis Club and another one out of town. We could make a couple hundred dollars a day. And quite a few people asked for me after the 1961 season, so I did pretty good."

∽

Mickey Mantle, another of Scott's clients who finished with 54 homers as a runner-up in the 1961 home run race, was conspicuously absent. The Yankees centerfielder was in Palm Springs, California, playing in the third annual Baseball Celebrity Golf Classic.

∽

The first newspaper announcement about the North Carolina Home Run Derby appeared as a small sidebar in the *Chicago Tribune* on September 28 with the headline, "Maris, Gentile, Killebrew to Tour in South" and listed the five cities and dates:

- Wilson, Sunday Oct. 15 @ Fleming Stadium
- Durham, Monday Oct. 16 @ Durham Athletic Park
- Greensboro, Tuesday Oct. 17 @ War Memorial Stadium
- Charlotte, Wednesday Oct. 18 @ Clark Griffith Park
- Winston-Salem, Thursday Oct. 19 @ Ernie Shore Stadium

The article provided this information, "The three sluggers will stage two-hour batting shows, hold autograph sessions between trips to the plate, and pose for pictures."

Bill Hunter of the *Times-News* (Burlington, North Carolina) wrote on October 10 tickets to the Home Run Derby, sponsored by the Carolina League, cost as much as $3.

THE BATTERY

One of the two pitchers throwing to the sluggers was 37-year-old Clyde King, a former big-league right-handed pitcher. King resided in North Carolina and managed the Rochester Red Wings of the International League in 1961.

Beginning in 1944, King spent seven years in the big leagues pitching for the Brooklyn Dodgers and the Cincinnati Reds. In his big-league career, King appeared in 200 games, winning 32 and losing 25, while posting an earned run average of 4.14.

Following his career in the big leagues, King returned to the minor leagues. In 1954 King pitched for the Triple-A Indianapolis Indians and the Double-A Tulsa Oilers, and in 1955 for the Double-A Atlanta Crackers. He then retired from pitching at the age of 31 and was named manager of the Atlanta Crackers on July 23, 1955. In 1956, the Crackers won the Southern Association pennant and playoffs.

The next year 1957 he managed the Hollywood Stars to a third-place finish in the Pacific Coast League.

His next managerial stop was for the 1958 Columbus (Ohio) Jets, who finished in fourth place in the International League.

The participants of the home run exhibition are (l to R) Roger Maris, "Chuck" Weatherspoon, Clyde King, Jim Gentile, Jack McKeon and Harmon Killebrew.

On August 3, 1959 King was hired to manage the Rochester Red Wings of the International League. He took over the managerial reins from Cot Deal, with the team finishing in fifth place.

Then, prior to the Rochester Red Wings' 1960 season, the team traveled to Cuba for spring training and opened the International League season in Havana on April 20, 1960, against the Havana Sugar Kings.

The game was delayed by 45 minutes, with the estimated crowd of 12,000 at Gran Stadium waiting for the late arrival of Cuba's prime minister Fidel Castro, scheduled to toss out the ceremonial first pitch. Moments before Castro took a theatrical wind-up to launch the season, he mentioned to King that the last time they were together was in 1947. That's when Castro pitched for Havana in an exhibition game against the Dodgers, with King was on the mound for Brooklyn.

Castro recalled that the University of Havana lost the game 13 years earlier but didn't remember the score.

King did, telling Castro, "The score was 15-1."

The other pitcher throwing to the visiting sluggers was 30-year-old right-hander Jack McKeon, manager of the Wilson Tobs. McKeon's professional baseball playing career began in 1949 as a catcher when he played for the minor-league Greenville Pirates of the Class D Alabama State League.

By 1955, though, the 24-year-old McKeon's playing career was coming to an end. He was player-manager for the Fayetteville Highlanders in the Carolina League. McKeon led the team to a 30-22 record during his two months as skipper.

Then, for three seasons, 1956-1958, McKeon managed and pitched for the Missoula (Montana) Timberjacks, a Washington Senators team in the Class C Pioneer League. (Future Hall of Famer Jim Kaat was part of the 1958 Timberjacks roster.) The jersey's design coincidently and appropriately was a green silhouette of a Northwest tree with the word "Jacks" prominently embodied across the chest, which might have appeared as if the team was named after and belonged to McKeon.

At the time, it was common for ballplayers in both the big leagues and minors to work a winter job to supplement their baseball salary. In the winter of 1958, for example, McKeon ran the Dugout Drive-in in Burlington, North Carolina, dishing out pizzas, pretzels and beer along with baseball talk.

In 1959 Jack managed the Fox Cities Foxes (Appleton, Wisconsin) in the Class B Three-I (Illinois-Indiana-Iowa) League.

Then, prior to the Wilson Tobs' 1960 season, Jack dropped "player" from his job description and was the team's manager and GM. He succeeded Jim Mills, who resigned after the 1959 season when Wilson had a 73-65 record and finished in second place.

In 1961, the Wilson Tobs were an affiliate of the Minnesota Twins after the Senators moved from Washington, D.C. to the

Twin Cities in the offseason. Jack led the minor-league team to a first-place finish with a record of 83-56.

"Being in baseball was a fun time," the 90-year-old McKeon said in 2021. He explained his team responsibilities were not confined to the field:

"In addition to being the manager, I was also the Tobs GM. I would sell the advertisements and get the promotions lined up and then when the season started, I was in the dugout managing the team." Those duties extended to the 1961 home run tour.

Catching duties for the five North Carolina events would be handled by a 29-year-old minor-league catcher, Charles "Chuck" Benny Weatherspoon, from Denny, Texas. Known as "Spoonie," he had played for the 1961 Wilson Tobs and led the team with 31 homers, 27 more than his next closest teammate. Weatherspoon had gained national attention that season when he became the first batter in professional baseball to hit seven grand slams in one season.

When Weatherspoon's name was mentioned, McKeon perked up, as Spoonie was an all-time favorite of his—Weatherspoon played for McKeon in Missoula, Fox Cities and Wilson.

"He was a big 6-foot 4-inch guy, and he was a lovable hunk. Not only did he play for me in Wilson, but in a bunch of places. We all got on him, playing pranks pretty good, though. You name it, we did it.

"Spoonie was a gem. He always used to lie about his age. One year, he'd say he was 30. The next year, he'd be 29.

"I had him in Missoula in the Pioneer League. Got him from the Giants. Bought him for $100. I carried him for about nine years. He was one of those guys that everyone wanted to room with him," McKeon recalled recently.

"I also signed his brother Clarence, who was an outfielder. We called him 'Little Spoon' and sometimes 'Tea Spoon.'"

PAYDAY

According to various published newspaper reports, the general consensus was that Killebrew and Gentile would each be paid $1,000 for every event they participated in (a total of $5,000), while Maris would receive $4,000 per event (a total of $20,000).

Contractual payment was to be made no matter who won the competition.

Years later, when this author asked Killebrew about the difference in their financial compensation for the derby, he replied: "Rog earned it. He was the star. Jim and I were the supporting players. People came to see the new home run king."

1961 MARATHON

Each slugger had to deal with the exhaustion factor from the long baseball season. Other than pride, there was no contractual incentive to win the home run contest.

Of the three, Maris had to be the most mentally and physically drained. After all, he had just endured the searing national spotlight and mounting pressure helping the Yankees win the pennant while also doing battle against the ghost of Babe Ruth for the home run record, ending the season with the World Series.

As evidence that baseball is a marathon, each player recorded the following games and plate appearances for the 1961 season:

- Maris appeared in 161 games and had 698 plate appearances, compared to his previous high of 136 games and 637 plate appearances in 1958.
- Killebrew saw action in 150 games with 656 plate appearances, compared to his previous high of 153 games and 648 plate appearances in 1959.

- Gentile played in 148 games with 601 plate appearances, compared to 1960 when he played in 138 games with 464 plate appearances.

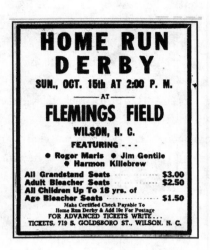

THE NORTH CAROLINA DERBY TOUR

In researching the five home run derby exhibitions, unfortunately, there were more than a few contradictions from newspaper accounts as to the number of homers each player hit, each player's compensation and per-game attendance.

Nonetheless, here for the first time is the most comprehensive account of those exhibitions that were an almost forgotten footnote to baseball's historic 1961 season.

Wilson, North Carolina
Sunday, October 15
Starting 2:30 p.m.

Fleming Stadium Dimensions: Left Field, 320; Center Field, 460; Right Field, 320
Ticket Prices: Grandstand, $3; bleacher adults, $2.50; children

under 18, $1.50. Although no price was publicized, there were 600 reserved chair seats on the field behind the players. **Attendance:** 1,200–2,500

Home Run Totals

- Killebrew: 20 homers
- Gentile: 15 homers
- Maris: 7 homers

The day before the first home run exhibition, Maris was scheduled to leave midnight Saturday, October 14 from Kansas City, Missouri. However, as a result of the worldwide civil defense exercise, "Sky Shield II," all commercial air traffic was grounded. His flight was rescheduled and took off at 6 a.m. Sunday.

Yet the local North Carolina newspapers implied Maris was at fault and reported it thusly, "He missed his flight out of Kansas City, where he lived during the winter, and spent several hours waiting for another flight."

Maris arrived at the Raleigh-Durham airport by way of Atlanta and was then flown in a private plane to Wilson just in time for the 2:30 p.m. Sunday appearance.

He later explained his poor showing with this: his timing was off as a result of not getting any sleep Saturday night, as his flight was delayed.

～

Roger's older brother by fifteen months, Rudy, accompanied him on this trip.

Newly crowned home run king Roger Maris connects for the North Carolina fans.

Fleming Stadium, the 1961 home of the Wilson Tobs, was the first of what would be five exhibitions.

The Tobs' ballpark opened in 1939 as Municipal Stadium, then renamed Fleming Stadium in June 1952 after Allie W. Fleming, one of Wilson's greatest benefactors of baseball, died a month earlier.

By 1961 the ballpark had seen its share of history. Six years earlier on September 14, 1955, a Grand Ole Opry All-Star Show concert was held in the ballpark featuring the Louvin Brothers, Cowboy Copas and a promising up-and-coming performer by the name of Elvis Presley. Tickets cost $1.25, rain or shine.

Then, in 1956, Ted Williams was the star attraction when the Red Sox played the Phillies in an exhibition game in early April. The "Thumper" delighted the overflow Fleming Stadium crowd with a two-run single to help Boston beat the Phils by a score of 6-4. (The ballpark still stands and is used for high-school and summer-collegiate baseball.)

Jim's Camera Center, located at 111 West Nash Street, took out a display ad in the local newspaper with the following pitch: "While you are getting your tickets, let us help you with your photographic needs. You will want to get good pictures of Roger Maris."

Outfield shaggers were Tobs second basemen Jim Burton, who played 108 games, batted .232 and cracked six homers in 1961. The other shagger was Benny Sinquefield, a former 1960 Wilson Tobs outfielder who retired after playing nine minor-league seasons, ending his career in 1960 with only 18 at-bats in eight games.

~

Participating in the exhibition provided McKeon another opportunity to earn a few bucks during the offseason while working for a wholesale house in Burlington.

In 2021 McKeon recalled that he and Clyde King were paid $100 to pitch in the five exhibitions. McKeon was also responsible for rounding up every baseball he could find in the state. In Wilson alone, it was reported that 15 dozen baseballs were either hit over the fence or fouled into the stands.

~

Although not competing against the three major leaguers, as a bonus local favorite Chuck Weatherspoon had two five-minute at-bats and cleared the left-field wall six times.

~

At the end of each exhibition, fans were invited down on to the field as Maris, Gentile and Killebrew lined up in different parts of the infield to sign autographs. There, fans could get close enough to marvel at Killebrew's massive muscular upper body, take note of Gentile's 6'3" height and Maris's almost sunken tired green eyes.

Fans line up on the field to get autographs from the three American League sluggers.

The local newspapers did note that Maris stood around for an hour after the show until everyone who wanted an autograph got it.

Charlie Hertlein was one of those kids to go on the field and snare each player's signature. Almost sixty years later he proudly recalls that the top of his head could be seen near the players in a local newspaper photo printed the next day.

The *Rocky Mount Telegram* of Rocky Mount, North Carolina, provided details of the home run derby stop at Fleming Stadium.

According to the story, 24 dozen official American League baseballs either went over the fence or were fouled off into the crowd. Due to the brisk 58-degree weather, the players wore turtleneck sweatshirts under their jerseys. Maris didn't wear stirrup socks but rather pulled his pants down near his ankles.

The accuracy of the article is in question, though, as it stated Maris was wearing Yankee road uniform No. 7 instead of No. 9, which was not true.

Rog broke two bats in his first four swings, which became souvenirs for a couple of youngsters.

One of Killebrew's homers travelled 490 feet and cleared the center-field fence by 35 feet. According to the AP report, this was the first homer in 21 years to clear the center-field fence.

~

The day after the trio of home run hitters performed at Fleming Stadium, Butch Lowery of the *Wilson Daily Times* reported on one of the questions asked of Maris, "Roger, how did you feel when number 61 sailed over the fence breaking Babe Ruth's old record?"

Roger's response was a simple, "Good."

Lowery pointed out in his article that one fan remarked that Maris went to bat with a sore hand after signing so many autographs.

The article described the crowd as "sardine-tight jammed retrievers" and that every long fly, home run or fence-banging ball was applauded with glee.

~

After the contest, Maris visited Governor Terry Sanford and his son at the governor's mansion and received a citation that proclaimed that Maris was a "North Carolina Good Egg."

~

Durham, North Carolina
Monday, October 16
Starting 7 p.m.

Durham Athletic Park Dimensions: Left Field, 360; Center Field, 460; Right Field, 296 (with a fence 30 feet high)
Ticket Prices: Unknown
Attendance: Estimated at 700 per the Associated Press or 1,200 by *The Sporting News*

Home Run Totals

- Maris: 12 homers
- Killebrew: 10 homers
- Gentile: 5 homers

In 2021, Gentile provided details about their Home Run Derby exhibition: "Originally, Frank Scott had us going to four towns but then he asked us to go to one more. So we went to Durham. It was cold that night, which must have kept the crowd numbers down.

"Everyone was friendly and very accommodating. Harmon and I got to go through the Reynolds tobacco factory on a guided tour. Killer and I didn't smoke but it was fun to see how they made cigarettes.

"I had a real good time."

As a result of not having calluses on his hands from swinging the bat the last couple of weeks, Gentile experienced hand blisters.

"I didn't use golf gloves when batting because I couldn't get the feel of the bat," he said. "I did use golf gloves inside my first baseman glove when it was hot, and it protected my glove from the sweat of my hand.

"I got a couple of blisters, like inside your thumb and index finger because I used a lot of pine tar, which didn't help because the skin on your hands got stuck on the bat. It didn't hurt that bad. I could swing the bat, but I was glad it was over after the fifth day."

After the exhibitions kids are invited on to the field to get autographs from Maris, Killebrew and Gentile.

~

The traveling party stayed at the Jack Tar Hotel in Durham, where in the afternoon a press conference was held. The players agreed that this was a novel barnstorming approach and enjoyed being in North Carolina.

~

Durham Athletic Park (DAP) was originally known as El Toro Park, opening in 1926. The name was changed to Durham Athletic Park after the 1933 baseball season. Longtime home of the Carolina League's Durham Bulls, the DAP is today best known as the setting for *Bull Durham*. Like Wilson Stadium, it still stands and is used for baseball.

~

Gene Warren of the *Greensboro Daily News* wrote that Gentile and Killebrew were in the dressing room 45 minutes before the event was to start. Maris—baseball's new home run monarch—arrived 15 minutes before the exhibition's start.

Maris was the last to hit, facing King. Maris was heckled by some fans, so he turned to them and held out his bat as if to infer for them to try it. No one stepped up to take his bat. He didn't hit one out until the 45th pitch, then he hit another.

Maris visited North Carolina Cerebral Palsy Hospital in Durham before the derby and was photographed autographing baseballs for four afflicted youngsters: Roy Pate, Vincent Locklear, Roy Faircloth and Terry Johnson. The kids were in attendance once the Derby began.

In *Durham Morning Herald* sports editor Jack Horner's Corner column, he quoted Maris' response to this question: Did he ever think he'd hit 61 home runs in a single season?

"Heck, no," he quoted Maris as saying. "I never dreamed of such a thing. In fact, the way I started out this season, I didn't think I'd hit 20 all year. I only hit three the first five weeks."

So how did he do it?

"It was just a question of getting the ball up," he explained. "When I met the ball squarely this year, I got the ball into the air more often than hitting line drives. It was that simple."

Maris then pointed at Killebrew, who slugged 46 home runs and said, "I'll bet Harm had 15 singles which would have gone for home runs had he gotten the balls up into the air."

Wearing golf gloves on both hands, Harmon Killebrew heads out to the field.

After the conclusion of the day's event, Gentile paid a visit to Watts Hospital for treatment of a hand blister.

After Wilson, Killebrew's hands began to blister. He found a pair of extra-large golf gloves at the Hillsdale Golf Club Monday after the press conference.

The next day in the *Durham Sun* newspaper, a photo of Tim Mico, Ronnie Roberts and Brad Evans posing with Maris appeared, along with an article by sportswriter Elton Casey, who had attended the press conference the previous day.

The article reported Maris took a few verbal pokes at inconsiderate fans and imaginative writers who, he claimed, had "put words in my mouth."

Specifically, Maris was quoted in the article as saying, "There were more stories made up about me last season than I ever heard of.

"Half the things I was credited with saying I never said. That burns me, to be quoted when I didn't say it. I don't like to have words put in my mouth."

Maris then gave an example: "Like the story about the 59th ball that I hit in Baltimore. There was all the stuff in the papers about me wanting the ball and what I thought of the fellow who got it and kept it. It was a case of writers making up something to put in the papers. That's all.

"I can get along with writers, sure, when they write just what I say. Nothing more.

"There are some of them, though, that I classify as 'rippers,' the guys that like to rip you apart."

Roger Maris gets a feel of his bat wearing golf gloves as he steps up to home plate that has foul lines chalked forming an "X."

When asked about the fans, Maris responded that some of them were all right, but that a good many were inconsiderate. He mentioned the interruptions he had endured when eating breakfast in a restaurant.

Then Maris was quoted about the "modern-day hitter."

"There is all this talk about the rabbit in the ball and a lot of other things. Credit, though, must be given to hitters now. Majority of people just don't want to give us credit as the players did years back.

"There may be more rabbit in the ball today, of course, but

there is a lot of good hitting, and players deserve to be commended. Their abilities shouldn't be questioned."

Then a reporter mentioned that the military may call up some big-league stars before next season and asked Maris how he stood, draft-wise.

Maris pulled out his wallet and read his Selective Service card: "I'm 1-D, meaning I'm married and have two kids."

Then he added with a smile, "Since this card was given to me, though, I have two more (children) to report."

It was announced this day by the Associated Press (AP) that the Yankees' Maris, Mantle, catcher Elston Howard and shortstop Tony Kubek were named to the AP All-Star starting team, while the Orioles' Jim Gentile made the second team.

Greensboro, North Carolina
Tuesday, October 17
Starting 8 p.m.

War Memorial Stadium Dimensions: Left Field, 327; Center Field, 401; Right Field, 327
Ticket Prices: Unknown
Attendance: 400

Home Run Totals

- Maris: 8 homers
- Killebrew: 7 homers
- Gentile: 4 homers

In the afternoon the three players visited the pediatric ward at Cone Hospital to sign autographs for an hour. When they heard one kid was in the emergency ward after an accident, they hurried down to see him.

~

Originally known as World War Memorial Stadium, the horseshoe-shaped venue was built in 1926 for both football and baseball. It served as long-time home to Minor League Baseball in Greensboro and is still in use as a ballpark, home to North Carolina A&T University baseball.

~

Gentile explained the derby event procedure. "We would sign autographs for about 20 minutes before the tournament. Then (Clyde) King or (Jack) McKeon would throw batting practice from the mound, not the grass in front of the mound. We would take about 10 swings to warm up.

"Once the contest began, we each had three five-minute at-bats, then signed more autographs."

~

In Earle Hellen's "Recording Sports" column for the Oct. 18 *Greensboro Record*, he wrote, "Last night Maris and his agent, Frank Scott, must have realized that the New York Yankee slugger is no super attraction to the baseball fans in Greensboro and other North Carolina minor league cities.

"Only around 500 to 600 fans showed up at Memorial Stadium.

"The promoters made their first mistake when they tried to

charge 'big city' prices. Greensboro's fans don't fall for that kind of bait. They usually want something for their money.

"In Maris' first at-bat, he was facing King. The Yankee slugger had trouble getting the ball in the air—just base knocks, line drives down the line, but he couldn't meet the ball properly to propel it over the walls. And that is what the fans came to see."

According to Hellen, Maris was given more chances to "win" the contest and did.

It took 45 pitches before he hit one over the fence.

King was quoted about the player's efforts, "They are trying so hard and that's throwing their timing off."

Maris, after watching Gentile get frustrated, said, "Look at Jim. He's mad as a hornet because he can't hit one. I'll be just as bad when I get up there."

Hellen wrote, "As a showman, Maris has a long way to go. He wasn't exactly surly as he has been described by some writers, but he wasn't a happy-appearing fellow. He had little to say to anyone."

Hellen estimated the Wilson crowd was "something around 1,500 or so."

~

Jack Elkins, a retired catcher who had played with Gentile on the Pueblo Dodgers in the Western League in 1953, came by to visit his old teammate.

~

In Hellen's Oct. 17 column in the *Greensboro Record*, he referenced Maris by writing, "If you visit Memorial Stadium tonight you'll be watching baseball's 'Man of the Year' and also the 'Sportsman of the Year.'"

He pointed out that Boston's Tracy Stallard, the pitcher who gave up Maris's home run number 61, was at one time a member of the Raleigh Caps and had pitched off the Memorial Stadium mound.

With blistered hands Jim Gentile sends a ball into the night.

In the second contest, *Greensboro Daily News* staff sportswriter Gene Warren had right-handed hitters Killebrew and Weatherspoon against lefties Maris and Gentile.

The southpaws won it 7-2, as Maris had four and Gentile hit three out, while Chuck Weatherspoon failed to connect.

According to Warren, the home run hitters lost 15 dozen baseballs in Wilson and eight dozen in Durham and added that while the players were signing autographs after the exhibition, one fan asked for all to hear, "Hey, Maris, let's see you smile." Though weary, he broke into a grin.

Maris and local lad Johnny Smith, the Greensboro Yankee batboy, pose for a photo keepsake.

Also reported in Warren's column was that Maris reportedly received $25,000 for appearing on Perry Como's *Kraft Music Hall* television show even though it was widely publicized that he was paid $7,500.

~

Johnny Smith, 14, was the Greensboro Yankees batboy in 1961. He lived only a couple blocks from the ballpark and in 2021 fondly recalled that he got his job by hanging around and helping with shining shoes and doing laundry.

As a result of being on the field with the players, Smith was fortunate to get his photo taken with Maris. Sixty years later he proudly displays it in his home.

~

Bob Godfrey was there that evening working as a vendor in the ballpark stands. In 2021 he shared his memories of the event:

"It was a cool, misty, dreary fall evening.

"McKeon pitched and his great Black catcher at Wilson, Chuck Weatherspoon, caught. (Black players were unusual in the Carolina League in19'61, though Wilson and McKeon had quite a few.)

"In the stands, some old leather-lung rode Maris all night. I didn't like it."

According to Godfrey, McKeon told him that he started throwing Maris water-logged balls out of the ball bag.

Godfrey recalls that, Maris stayed for long line of autograph seekers afterward.

"I worked as vendor to make a few bucks. Sold peanuts and popcorn, as that was a good way to get in free. I was paid 10 percent of my sales. If I sold a total of $10, I'd make a dollar.

"The tickets to the Derby were too high for me, probably around $5."

With a guesstimate, Godfrey said, "The crowd that night must have been about 500-700."

Charlotte, North Carolina,
Wednesday October 18
7:45 p.m.

Clark Griffith Park Dimensions: Left Field, 320; Center Field, 390; Right Field, 320
Ticket Prices: Adults $2, Children $1.50
Attendance: 616

Home Run Totals

- Killebrew: 9 homers
- Maris: 8 homers
- Gentile: 8 homers

Clark Griffith Park opened in 1941 by Washington Senators owner Clark Griffith to house his Class B Charlotte Hornets. Future Minnesota Twins owner Calvin Griffith ran the team on behalf of his uncle. It was later renovated for a Baltimore Orioles farm team run by the always-colorful Jim Crockett, a wrestling promoter know for employing pro grapplers on the grounds crew. Alas, the ballpark burned down in 1985.

Gentile explained the local media's focus: "The newspaper guys wanted to talk to Roger, not so much Killebrew or me."

HARMON KILLEBREW   **ROGER MARIS**   **JIM GENTILE**

MEET! SEE! IN PERSON
☆ Roger Maris

★ Home Run Hitting Sensation of N. Y. Yankees
   ● Hit 61 Home Runs—New Major League Record
★ Jim Gentile 46 HR's   ★ Harmon Killebrew 46 HR's
   (Baltimore Blaster)   (Minnesota Mauler)

IN

World Series - Home Run Derby

★ Don't miss this once-in-a-lifetime opportunity to see the world's greatest home run hitters in a 2-hour home run hitting derby. Including pauses between trips to the plate for Autograph Sessions, Answering Questions from Stands, Posing for Pictures.   ● Autograph Pictures Available

Wednesday, Oct. 18 - 7:45 P.M. Gates Open 6:45
CLARK GRIFFITH PARK, CHARLOTTE, N. C.

SPECIAL PRICES!   ADULTS **2.00**   CHILDREN **1.50**

(All Tickets Incl. Tax)

In 1961 boys wanted to grow up and be an astronaut like Alan Shepard
or a major league baseball player like Roger Maris.

Gentile continued, "Maris was Mr. Baseball. Hit 61 home runs."

Gentile quoted Maris's response to a series of questions, "Roger said, 'If I knew you were going to ask me all these same old questions, I would have brought a tape recorder and played it for you.' Well, that got in the paper and cut everything down."

In an *El Paso Herald Post* (Texas) article dated October 21, Joe Williams wrote that the Charlotte club president introduced Maris to an elderly resident named Jerry Ball, who claimed to have the 44-ounce bat that Babe Ruth used to hit home runs Nos. 57, 58, and 59 in 1921.

Maris used the bat for his first ten swings and hit three out, one of which Frank Scott said, "Would have been a home run in any park, anywhere."

When asked about the bat, Roger was quoted, "The bat's too heavy for me, and not my size."

He added after the exhibition: "I had difficulty swinging it or meeting the ball. [But] if I had to use it [during the season], I think I'd get my share."

∿

The *Montana Standard* ran a wire service sidebar with a conflicting attendance number of only 61, not 616. As a result, the *Indianapolis Star* ran a sidebar headline: "61 PAY TO SEE SLUGGERS!" Or maybe it was the other way around.

∿

The Associated Press reported that Gentile complained about cheap baseballs being used, which were the same balls used in the Class-B Carolina League.

Gentile was quoted, "I don't believe they are [the same Class-B baseballs]. You have to swing like heck to keep from making a fool of yourself."

Maris agreed: "You get real good wood on them and they die."

McKeon and King, the catcher and pitcher for the derby, declined to comment.

~

In the October 19 *Charlotte Observer*, sportswriter Herman Helms posed this question to Killebrew: how long will Roger Maris' 61 home runs stand? "It's my feeling that it will be in the books for a good many years," declared Killebrew.

"I'm taking nothing away from Roger, but it surprised me the number of good pitches which he got to hit. That isn't likely to be the case for him next season."

~

In the same edition Gentile was interviewed and talked about the role that Hoyt Wilhelm of Charlotte and Skinny Brown of Greensboro played for the Orioles in 1961.

First, he talked about Hoyt, who appeared in 52 games as a relief pitcher: "He did a heck of a job for us, but we had to use him entirely too much."

Then he mentioned the possibility that Skinny "might be moved to the bullpen to lighten the load for Hoyt next season."

~

In the October 19 *Charlotte Observer* sportswriter Dick Pierce quoted Killebrew that the most attractive thing to the attending fans have been the autograph sessions "It's getting to where my hand fits a ball-point pen better than it does a 35-inch bat," he said with a laugh.

~

In an attempt to provide answers about poor attendance and the lack of long balls, Herman Helms quoted Gentile: "We haven't been drawing good crowds and I know that the man who's promoting this thing isn't making any money. But the baseballs he's been giving us to hit must be 97-cent jobs.

"It's ridiculous. You don't want to stand up there and make a fool of yourself, so you swing so hard that you're exposing yourself to injury. You hit the heck out of them, and they won't go anyplace. I've torn my hands up trying to keep from making a fool of myself."

Maris agreed, "You get good wood on them and they take off pretty good, then all of a sudden they die."

"They told us the balls we would use would be the same as they use in the Carolina League," said Gentile. "But you can't tell me that any organized baseball league would use balls like these."

~

Winston-Salem, North Carolina
Thursday, October 19
Starting 7 p.m.

Ernie Shore Field: Dimensions: Left Field, 335; Center Field, 400; Right Field, 335
Ticket Prices: Unknown
Attendance: 489
Home Run Totals

- Killebrew: 9 homers
- Maris: 7 homers
- ·Gentile: 4 homers

Ernie Shore Field opened in 1956. It was named after the pitcher who was part of baseball's most unique perfect game on June 23, 1917. Babe Ruth was starting pitcher for the Boston Red Sox against the Washington Senators. His first four pitches to leadoff batter Ray Morgan were called balls by umpire Brick Owens. Ruth argued and was thrown out of the game.

Shore came in to replace Ruth on the mound, and Owens was thrown out trying to steal. Shore retired the next 26 batters to throw the fourth perfect game in major league history's modern era. (Today this would not be considered a perfect game, as a runner did indeed reach first base.) At the time of the Home Run Derby, Shore was the sheriff of Forsyth County.

Ernie Shore Field still stands: the longtime home to Minor League Baseball in Winston-Salem is now David F. Couch Ballpark, home to the Wake Forest Demon Deacons baseball program.

Maris was the first player to step into the batter's box at Ernie Shore Field. According to Carlton Byrd, sports editor of the *Twin City Sentinel*, he topped the first pitch, sending it down the first-base line. With that grounder, Jim Gentile started singing "You Used to Be a Beautiful Baby" loud enough to go over the public-address system, evoking laughter from those in attendance.

Gentile explained what happened after he set foot in the batter's box: "Jack and Clyde would throw so many pitches for about five minutes, then the next would take over. So, for the first round, I might face McKeon and then King in the second round."

Gentile struggled. "The baseballs they used were like rocks. If it didn't go out, it didn't go out."

The pitch never reaches catcher Chuck Weatherspoon as the Killer nails another baseball.

Gentile and Killebrew made some new friends on this trip, as McKeon recalls. "Chuck Weatherspoon was a very nice gentleman," he said in 2021. "He could hit. He came with Killer and me a couple times for dinner at a local steakhouse."

McKeon thought that the reason the derbies didn't draw bigger crowds was because of the fall weather. "The weather was cool and it was football season down there, so the high schools are playing football. It didn't go over as well as everyone thought it would, but we had a lot of fun. The players signed a lot of autographs."

He thought Maris might have been burnt out after the past season: "I think he just wanted get it over with and go home."

McKeon, never at a loss for a good story, shared this 1950s experience in 2021 about Weatherspoon, catcher for most of the Home Run Derbies when he wasn't hitting back in October 1961.

"When I managed the Missoula club in 1958, I found out that Chuck Weatherspoon was deathly afraid of any and all reptiles. Well, that's all his teammates needed to hear. Jim Kaat was on that club, and he would find lizards and put 'em in Spoonie's jock hanging in the clubhouse.

"But most of all, Spoonie was afraid of snakes like nobody's business.

"One night in 1961 we were playing the Raleigh Capitals club in Devereux Meadow. We already won the pennant. Enos Slaughter was their manager.

"There was an article in the paper that Gates Brown of the Durham Bulls found a snake while playing right field.

"So, I tell the Raleigh club's first-base coach to tell their right fielder to tell Spoonie to be careful of the snakes. Next thing I looked up we had two second basemen. Weatherspoon wouldn't go out to right field.

"I called time. I finally convinced him to go out and play right field.

"Once I was back in the dugout, I began rounding up all the small rocks around the dugout I could and gave them to my centerfielder Roberto Tanno. I told him to move closer to right field and without getting caught, toss rocks behind Spoonie.

"Well, as soon as Spoonie heard the pebbles fly by and land in the grass here he comes running in and says, "Skip, look, I'll play any place else, but I ain't going back out there."

"Once I got him back in right field again, you had to see him playing the position for the rest of the game. He'd have his hands on his knees but would be looking over his shoulders for snakes and wouldn't watch the pitcher or batter.

"If a ball was hit out there, for sure it would be a triple.

"Spoonie was the best."

~

For a summary of the home run derby, the *Hartford Courant* ran a headline: "Killebrew Clouts Homers Profusely."

~

Sport fans are at the mercy of official scorers and reporters to accurately keep statistics of sporting events.

Heading into the last Derby at Ernie Shore Field, the total number of homers hit by each player as reported in multiple newspapers was: Killebrew forty-six, Maris thirty-five and Gentile thirty-two.

Frank Spencer, a sportswriter for the *Twin City Sentinel*, Winston-Salem's afternoon newspaper, wrote an article for the October 20 edition that included the number of homers hit by each player at Ernie Shore Field the previous night. In the article Spencer noted that Killebrew had 9, Maris clouted 7 and Gentile slammed 4. Other than Killebrew's homers, those numbers when added to Maris and Gentile's totals for the previous four exhibition numbers do not reflect the final total number of homers hit as compiled by the Associated Press and printed in *The Sporting News*: Killebrew clouted fifty-five, Maris belted forty-six and Gentile smacked thirty-nine.

~

In Spencer's article, one of the promoters who was not identified was quoted, "If Roger Maris was in a booth at the

State Fair he would have attracted many thousands of fans. What this tour has proved is that they want to see him and touch him and get his autograph, not to see him hit. But they don't know what they missed by not seeing hit that ball. He's a great youngster and just as great a ballplayer as the records show."

≈

According to a newspaper footnote, approximately 450 baseballs were used for practice, autographs and the contest.

≈

In an *El Paso Herald Post* article dated October 21, Joe Williams wrote a column titled "Maris and Troupe Lay Egg in N.C."

In the article, Williams quoted Frank Scott responding to Williams' statement that the derby was a failure: "By Broadway's definition, it was a turkey. Our largest turnout was 220. The others were below 1,000, so on that basis it wasn't exactly a smash hit."

It appears that the newspaper typesetter dropped some zeroes in the total attendance. It probably should have been 2,200—not 220—based on information in other newspaper accounts. As a result of various newspaper articles pertaining to the five 1961 Home Run Derby exhibitions in North Carolina, there are factual discrepancies, probably exaggerations and maybe even fabrications, so it's hard to know which ones to discard and which to keep.

The columnist further stated that the idea of the Home Run Derby belonged to Matt Boykin, the president of the Wilson Tobs, and that Maris earned $16,000 (other accounts cited $20,000), while Killebrew and Gentile each received $4,000.

According to Williams, Scott, the business manager, later

revealed: "The day we were to open in Wilson, some of the townies warned us we wouldn't draw at the ballpark. They told us people had simply stopped going there."

POST GAME

Just a few months shy of the 60th anniversary, Gentile mentioned that one of the best benefits of the 1961 Home Run Derby was his newfound friendship with Harmon Killebrew.

"I really got to know Killebrew," Gentile said. "After it was over, he drove back to Baltimore with me in the new white Corvette given to me at the end of the season on a night I was honored at the ballpark by the Baltimore fans.

"Killer spent the night at my house and then I dropped him off at the airport. We became very good friends. He was one helluva hitter, that guy, for home runs.

"I also remember that the family of Matt Boykin had us to his house for dinner. Met his family, wonderful people. Back then, there was only one big-league game on TV.

"It was on Saturdays with (Dizzy) Dean, (Buddy) Blattner and (Pee Wee) Reese. I think that's why he wanted to bring us down there. People wanted to see home run hitters. I don't know if we got him enough money back in the venture."

There were a couple of local North Carolina newspaper writers not pleased with the way in which Maris conducted himself and so informed their readers.

Maris was unprepared for a series of unpredictable circumstances that he experienced in 1961—both mentally and physical challenging—by the time he landed in North Carolina on October 15. Without defending or explaining, but rather just noting, here are those circumstances and situations he faced from March until October of 1961:

Roger and his wife, Pat, who was pregnant with their fourth child, decided they would drive with their three children from Raytown, Missouri to St. Petersburg, Florida as a little vacation prior to spring training.

Unfortunately, their car broke down in rural Georgia.

As a result, they had to be towed for miles over bumpy roads. Eventually they made it to St. Petersburg, but as a result of the rough road ride, Pat experienced pregnancy complications and went to the local hospital. So, before Maris could break a sweat in spring training in 1961, he was worried and concerned about his wife and unborn baby.

Once the baseball season began, Maris joined his teammates in dealing with daily challenges that involved facing curveballs, fast balls, change-ups and screwballs.

But for the 1961 season, the Yankee players and coaches also needed to adapt to a new manager, Ralph Houk.

Over the course of six months of playing baseball, the weather conditions ranged from temperatures below 40 degrees to over 100 degrees with always a chance of rain.

Playing day games after night games was common. Same with playing in-season exhibition games, such as the April 14 exhibition against the cadets at West Point.

Traveling in 1961 now included round-trip flights to the West Coast for the first time in the American League history to play the expansion Los Angeles Angels. That also resulted in competing against the nine other teams in an expanded schedule, all the while trying to win the pennant.

Coming off his 1960 MVP season, Maris was in high demand with sportswriters, doing countless interviews before and after games.

Trying to find his rhythm and focus, Maris struggled at the

plate and by the middle of May, he had a batting average of .228, with only 3 homers and 10 RBI.

Yankees management, thinking that Maris's vision was not 100 percent, arranged for him to see an eye specialist on May 22. The exam didn't find any optical problems, but to make matters worse, Maris experienced vision problems by misusing a prescribed eye-bathing solution, causing him to come out of that night's game.

In the middle of July, commissioner Ford Frick imposed a 154-game deadline to break baseball's most hallowed single-season record of 60 home runs in a season, as that record was set by Babe Ruth in 1927 during a 154-game season.

Between Maris's participation in two All-Star Games, on July 10 at San Francisco and July 30 at Boston, he played in a July 24 exhibition game at Yankee Stadium against the San Francisco Giants.

However, during the next day's doubleheader, he cracked four home runs, bringing his total to 40 homers for the season, placing him 24 games ahead of Ruth's record pace.

As his home-run totals rose, Maris was besieged with a myriad of business opportunities that included endorsements and public appearances, including at a batting cage in Brooklyn.

By August, fans everywhere were taking sides between Mantle and Maris as to who they most wanted to break the record. It appeared that in most newspapers across America, Maris was coming in a distant second.

On August 2, Yankees co-owner Del Webb joined the fans' voting preference by publicly favoring Mantle.

The August 4 edition of the *Herald-News* newspaper of Passaic, N.J., ran an article with the headline "READERS FAVOR MANTLE." The story explained that 80 percent of respondents predicted that Mantle was the mathematical favorite to break Ruth's hallowed record of 60 homers.

Along with Mantle, Maris was provided the honor of posing

for a *LIFE* magazine cover that hit newsstands by mid-August, as this was no longer just a New York sports story.

Amidst all this, Maris experienced the disappointment and frustration of being on the road when his son was born between him hitting his 49th and 50th home runs. He did, however, manage to squeeze in a filmed cameo with Mantle and Yogi Berra for a Hollywood movie, *That Touch of Mink*, starring Cary Grant and Doris Day, set for release in early 1962.

Newsweek climbed aboard the home-run bandwagon with a front-page story in its Aug. 14, 1961 issue, titled "Home Run Year Target 60."

Media coverage became more intense and unrelenting, to the point where Maris experienced the loss of clumps of scalp hair—the result of stress, said his doctor.

In September, along with Mantle, Maris taped an appearance on Perry Como's *Kraft Music Hour*, scheduled to air on national TV after the regular season concluded.

Bringing more attention to himself, Rog got into a well-publicized headline squabble about the strike zone with umpire Hank Soar on September 12.

In addition to being scrutinized by the hordes of media, including one prominent New York sportswriter dissatisfied with writing about the on-field game story and instead began writing personal attacks of Maris. The media swarm conducted interviews before and after games, and would on occasion write falsehoods about Roger's personal life. This includes impromptu interviews taking place mere moments after home run No. 59 hit the seats in Baltimore's Memorial Stadium.

That homer and the next two Maris hit meant that he was actually being interviewed while the game was still in progress.

Then there was the brouhaha with a Baltimore fan who recovered home run No. 59 and began to negotiate through the media about what he wanted from Maris in exchange for grabbing the ball.

All the while, Maris, along with his Yankee teammates, was trying to win the American League pennant. Eventually, the regular season concluded and the second and most important baseball season—the post-season—began.

In the best-of-seven series, Maris was in the lineup but was completely spent having endured the last eight months that began with his car breaking down in Georgia.

~

The Sporting News Nov. 1, 1961 edition summarized the North Carolina exhibition as a financial flop. One source estimated the loss as high as $20,000.

The baseball newspaper had the payouts for each player. Maris was paid $16,000, while Gentile and Killebrew received $4,000 each.

It also listed the attendance:

Wilson 2,500
Durham 1,200 (Not the 700 that was reported by the Associated Press)
Greensboro 400
Charlotte 616
Winston-Salem 489

It noted that the financial backer of the derby was J. Norris Barnes, an Elm City, North Carolina, businessman who told *The Sporting News*, "All I can tell you," he said, "is that we didn't make any money."

He also estimated that 450 balls were used for the events.

Reflecting on all that happened over those five Home Run Derbies in North Carolina, in 2021 Jim Gentile summarized his experience this way:

"It was my second year in the big leagues. It was a great

experience. The people down there treated us great. It was one of the best experiences I ever had. They cheered for Roger, Killer and me. It was fun.

"That's baseball."

"Maris is a living symbol of the strong, silent type of athlete," wrote *Charlotte Observer* sportswriter Herman Helms in his October 17 column. "He prefers not to discuss other players for fear that there will be misunderstanding and he may be accused of criticizing them. He does not like to talk of his own accomplishments because he is not a gloater."

Poetically Helms wrote of Maris's desire to be with his family and privacy, "Clear the roads which lead to his home. Grant him the peace which can only be found at his own fireside."

The day after the five-city North Carolina Home Run Derby concluded Maris boarded a plane for Omaha, Nebraska, where he would team up with golf pro Dick Knight against pro Don January and Olympic athlete Johnny Weissmuller at the Miracle Hill Links in an October 21 celebrity golf exhibition. Maris shot a 93 and then was on his way to begin an exhausting rubber-chicken circuit, collecting awards, plaques and honors for the just-concluded 1961 baseball season.

Chapter 7

Behind The Seams Home Run Tales

Myth buster: baseball wasn't invented or even discovered by Abner Doubleday. Instead, it evolved. In fact, Cooperstown isn't the birthplace of baseball. It is more of a spiritual home.

Point is, evolution takes shape in many ways long before something becomes established. I'm convinced that what took place when the San Diego Padres hosted the 1978 All-Star Game played a significant role in many now popular All-Star Game events and promotions. Some worked, others didn't. Still others were simply ahead of their time.

Players competing against each other to see who could hit the most home runs probably began the same day that a person batted a ball. But the story of the All-Star Game Home Run Derby got a huge boost when we decided to open the player workouts to the general public for the first time.

As Padres promotion director, earlier that year I had realized that when retired players play in an Old Timers game, the excitement of the event usually fades soon after the introductions. More often than not, the actual three-inning game turned out to be a disappointing affair, played in slow motion due to the ages of the players and their clearly diminished skills.

The one aspect of baseball that all players (except for some pitchers) enjoy is hitting a baseball thrown much slower than what they experienced in their careers. So I decided that to ensure that the hitters could reach the seats that I would have special baseballs manufactured. These baseballs were guaranteed to travel 25 percent further when hit, an adjustment that would help the long ball become a very long ball.

On June 18, 1978, we held an Old Timers Game featuring former Major League All-Stars vs. former San Diego Padres. The teams included sluggers Willie Mays, Eddie Mathews, Nate Colbert and Al Ferrara.

I don't remember who won the contest but three weeks later, on July 10, 1978—the annual All-Star Game workout—the unused baseballs from the Padres Old Timers Game came into play again.

One of the Padres coaches, Whitey Wietelmann, had about six dozen of the highly compressed "rabbit baseballs," rat-holed from that Old Timers Game. Without saying a word to anybody, Whitey made sure the National League hitters were served up the special balls during their batting practice.

As the American Leaguers looked on in bewildered amazement, one National League hitter after another crushed the pitches deep into the stands. When it was the AL's turn in the batting cage, the regular National League baseballs were used and many landed in the deep outfield with only a few hitting the seats. Whitey revealed his secret much later and with a twinkling grin.

From that little baseball adjustment by Whitey, those fans who came for the All-Star Game workout were treated to a show unlike any before and helped spawn the long-ball hitting contests now an integral part of the annual All-Star Game festivities.

During the 1977 season Kingman played for the San Diego Padres, New York Mets, California Angels and New York Yankees.

1979 Dave Kingman

Power-hitting outfielder Dave Kingman squeezed in a cup-of-coffee stay with the Padres in 1977 when he appeared in 56 games. That was the season "Sky King" also played for the Mets, Angels and Yankees.

During his brief San Diego stay, I developed a casual friendship with the slugger.

It was long enough for me to ask him two years later if he would participate in a June 15, 1979, Padres pre-game home run derby when he was with the Cubs.

After negotiating his participation fee—a fishing rod and reel—he agreed.

Relaxing in the dugout moments before the 1978 All-Star introductions begin are (L to R) Willie Stargell, Jack Clark, Dave Winfield and Rollie Fingers. (Photo by Fred O. Rodgers)

The other participants were Dave Winfield, Willie Mays, Eddie Mathews and Doug Rader. The moundsmen lineup included Chuck Estrada, Bob Feller, Warren Spahn and Whitey Ford.

I was in the corner of the dugout watching Mathews' at-bat in which he only hit grounders. Eddie's efforts worried me, as I had requested the pitchers throw nothing but gopher balls to help the sluggers reach the seats.

At that moment, Ford must have detected my concern because he came up behind me and boastfully said to the back of my head so that I could hear him, "No one is going to get even a weak grounder off me when I'm out there. I'm gonna strike 'em all out."

At that moment, a photographer snapped our picture that captured my expression of speechless dismay.

When Kingman stepped up to the plate to face Ford, I now expected Whitey to throw nothing but junk, which was sure to frustrate Dave.

It was just the opposite. The crafty Yankee left-hander gave "King Kong" nothing but fat fastballs right down the #@*%.

Kingman blasted one of them into the unoccupied, 50-yard-line San Diego Chargers press level sky box in left field, becoming the first player to ever reach the stadium's third level.

As the fans went crazy, realizing they had just witnessed the farthest ball ever hit in San Diego Stadium history, I shot a glance at Whitey still on the mound. He had a devilish smile looking at me that I took as "Happy now?"

Big Dave Winfield out-homered Kingman 6-5 to win the derby, as Willie Mays managed to hit three out while Rader and Mathews were shut out.

Eventually, Chicago played the Padres in the real game. Kingman hit his 21st homer of the season off Eric Rasmussen to help the Cubbies beat the Padres 3-2.

1980 Hank Aaron

After the Padres 1979 Old Timers game, I couldn't help but think about Yogi Berra's insightful marketing dictum, "You can observe a lot by just watching."

It was obvious to me that watching an old-timer stumble

after grounders, another grab their shoulder after making a throw, two players muffing what used to be an easy play on a lazy fly ball when they were in their prime and most players huffing and puffing to first base, was not easy.

Moments before the Padres Home Run Derby Andy Strasberg shares smiles with Hank Aaron. In the background is former Red Sox star Dick Stuart, Bucs manager Chuck Tanner and Jim Bunning sitting on the bench. (Photo by Fred O. Rodgers)

My challenge in trying to assemble two Old Timers teams was finding enough not-too-old former players whom fans would be interested in seeing once again, plus enough players who could and wanted to play each specific position.

Not surprisingly, finding retired catchers who could squat, catch, throw, bat and run was always a problem. Especially, squat.

Acutely aware that my job was to generate revenue with special promotions and save the team money, I decided to reduce the 1980 Old Timers game down to the basics—a pitcher throwing to hitters and hitters trying to hit the crap out of the ball.

In other words, a home run derby.

I began to put pen to paper so that I could present it to my boss and get approval.

Andy Strasberg standing with Harmon Killebrew. (Photo by Fred O. Rodgers)

Instead of two rosters totaling 35 players there would be a couple of former "name" pitching greats and a few big-time sluggers from the recent past. That formula would result in a significant cost savings, while also selling tickets and, I hoped, generating *oohs* and *aahs* from fans.

To reduce expenses even more, I would mix some current players in the contest.

Knowing that our GM, Bob Fontaine, had been a scout for the Pirates for 18 seasons going back to 1951, I asked him if he could entice his long-time friends Willie Stargell and Dave Parker to try to park some balls in the seats before the regularly scheduled Padres game when the Pirates were in town.

Not only did Fontaine tell me he would do it, he told me he could also get former Pirates first baseman Dick Stuart, who hit 66 homers one season in the minors back in 1956.

I selected May 11, 1980, for the contest when the Buccos were in town.

For the Padres, I would invite Gene Tenace and Dave Winfield, though he later politely declined to take part. Knowing this ensemble needed a headliner, my plan was to reach out to baseball's all-time home run king, Hank Aaron.

The mound chuckers would be Jim Bunning, Warren Spahn and our pitching coach, Chuck Estrada.

In memo form, I presented my proposal to Padres VP Business Elten Schiller for his approval. On the spot, he reviewed it and said, "Great concept," and then asked, "How do you plan to invite Hank Aaron?"

Well, that was an odd question because he knew that, as I had done before with other Old Timers game invitees, I would simply send a letter of invitation.

Schiller offered me some advice: "You can't invite Hank Aaron by letter. Show him the respect he has earned. You need to fly to Atlanta and ask him in person."

That's exactly what I did.

A couple of weeks later, I was ushered into Hank's Atlanta-Fulton County Stadium office, as he was the Braves' director of player development. Right off the bat, he started the conversation by asking me what had brought me to Atlanta.

First, I said, "Thanks for taking the time to see me."

Then got right to the point, "I'd like to invite you to our home run hitting contest next season before a Padres game."

Home Run King Hank Aaron faces Warren Spahn, the winningest left hander in MLB history. Padres bullpen catcher Lenny Arevalo is behind the plate. (Photo by Fred O. Rodgers)

Aaron seemed flabbergasted and quizzed me, "You flew out here from San Diego to invite me to a home run hitting contest before a Padres game?"

"I did, and I'm hoping that your calendar is free the weekend of May 11 next season."

Aaron asked about the format and who else would be participating.

I mentioned the roster of sluggers and explained that each batter would have three at-bats of seven swings each. As I explained, it would be "a total of 21 swings, so it's a homer or nothing."

Then I shared with Aaron that the pitchers would be Bunning, Spahn and Chuck Estrada.

Before I could continue, Aaron casually mentioned that Spahn would never agree to participate.

"He's already responded with a yes," I replied. "As you know, Warren is the minor league pitching coach for the California

Angels, so I asked Angels president Buzzie Bavasi, who I used to work for, to make those arrangements and he did."

In disbelief, Aaron uttered, "Uh, huh," though with a smile.

He then said what I was hoping to hear, "Okay, since you flew out here all the way from San Diego, I can't turn down your invitation."

I wanted to jump up and hug the "Hammer," but instead I cordially said in my grown-up voice, "Thank you."

Then, in a business-like manner, I explained, "I will coordinate details with your office."

I politely excused myself and left the ballpark happy dancing in my head through the parking lot.

That weekend in early May, when Hank's plane touched down in San Diego, I was there to personally greet him at the airport and escort him to his hotel.

The morning of the contest, I was thrilled to see Aaron walking around the field in his Atlanta Braves uniform. I swear he looked like he could still play both ends of a twin-bill.

I stood in the corner of the visitors' dugout as the derby was taking place. If an issue of any kind arose, I wanted to be there to solve it.

When Aaron was about to take his first turn at the plate, rather than stand in the on-deck circle, he approached me. He mentioned that his back was aching and that he didn't think he could reach the warning track. I politely smiled.

But Hank Aaron didn't disappoint. Even with a bad back in his first two at bats, his wrists deposited four baseballs into the left-field bleachers.

Then, moments before his third and last at-bat, I watched Hank step into the batter's box against Warren Spahn, knowing that he was seven swings from finishing.

I wondered if the fans in the ballpark realized what they were witnessing. Here was the player who had hit the most career homers facing the pitcher who had the most wins for left-handers.

Two baseball legends who at one time were teammates. Secretly, I was pleased with myself that I made this match-up happen. But that pride was short-lived as the left-hander's first pitch was a brush-back, which was obviously not appreciated by Hank.

Immediately, I thought about Spahn's well-known approach to facing hitters back in the day, "Hitting is timing. Pitching is upsetting timing."

The next pitch was a screwball that must have been recognized by Hank because it comes in looking like a strike, then brakes low and away. At that, Hank was done. He prematurely ended the derby by simply walking back to the dugout.

I understood and was equally frustrated and disappointed with Spahn's performance.

The derby winner was Willie Stargell. Second guessing myself on the chance that "Pops" won the contest I should have had a taped recording of Pirates broadcaster Bob Prince on standby so we could have played "The Gunner's" call over the PA.

"And it's chicken on the hill with Will!"

Then it was time for the current players to take the field.

The Padres' Randy Jones blanked the Pirates and won with five San Diego runners crossing the plate. Our attendance for the game was 22,522, which was somewhat better than our average of 21,465 to that point on the season.

In the real game, I paid close attention to how the derby contestants who were not retired did, knowing that their participation in a home run hitting contest might be the excuse they would use because it ruined their swing.

For the record, Parker went 0-for-4 and Tenace had a hit in four at-bats. Stargell did not play.

Willie Stargell takes his Home Run Derby cuts as onlookers Andy Strasberg (kneeling), Al Schuss (PCL Padres radio announcer) keeps score and Padres PA announcer Bruce Binkowski keeps the fans informed. (Photo by Fred O. Rodgers)

The next morning, I drove Aaron to the airport.

Immediately, I thanked him again for making the trip and participating in the derby. I wanted to bring up what had happened in his last at bat against Spahn but chickened out.

It was quiet as we traveled on the freeway to San Diego's Lindbergh Field.

Then Hank startled me by motioning with his left hand in front of his left shoulder twisting his hand so that his palm was facing away from his body as if he was throwing a screwball.

He said, "He's still a fierce competitor."

That he is.

1983 Terry Kennedy

Fortunately, I was the recipient of trust from many Padre players while working for the team. As an added benefit, some of them understood and appreciated my sense of humor. One such player was Terry Kennedy, who caught for the Padres from 1981 to 1986.

"TK" was one of my go-to guys when I needed something more than a player signing an autograph for a kid before a game.

As one example, there was the time Terry agreed to let me sneak in behind his bat for his baseball card shoot.

Or when I persuaded Terry to get dressed in an oversize cap, buggy eyes, and large bow tie for a Padres TV commercial.

During his Padres years (1981-1986) Terry Kennedy hit more doubles than homers each season.

Then there was the time Terry participated in a pre-game home run derby contest.

Others in the contest included Nate Colbert, Bob Watson (a last-minute replacement for the injured Steve Garvey), Harmon Killebrew and Dale Murphy.

While Kennedy was more of a doubles hitter than home run basher, on that day he put on a show.

First, TK enlisted the help of Padres coach and clubhouse man Whitey Wietelmann to make specific adjustments to the bat he would use in the contest. Whitey carefully drilled a hole in it from the top down about six inches and then filled it with cork.

"TK" had a big league sense of humor who was a willing candidate to participate in Padres marketing ideas.

This made the bat lighter and thus faster to get through the strike zone when hitting a baseball. Once in the batter's box with his loaded lumber, Kennedy took a hop step towards the pitched ball to get extra momentum. The results brought the crowd to their feet as the baseball sailed between the scoreboard and light tower and into the parking lot.

It was the first time that anyone could remember a ball being hit clear out of San Diego Stadium.

1992 All-Star Game HR Derby

The 1992 MLB Home Run Derby at Jack Murphy Stadium the day before the All-Star Game was going to be memorable for those fans sitting in the right-field stands.

Some of the game's best sluggers at the time were competing, including Ken Griffey Jr., Mark McGwire, Cal Ripken Jr., Larry Walker, Gary Sheffield, Fred McGriff and Barry Bonds.

There was one extra added surprise attraction—Cheryl Smith, who was in her twenties, working in the Padres front office, would be in the outfield that day.

Cheryl Smith-Lemox playing right field at Jack Murphy Stadium during the 1992 All-Star Game Home Run Derby. She entertained the fans with her fielding skills. (Photo by Larry Carpa.)

During the competition a few shaggers would be in the field to throw back those baseballs that didn't reach the stands. Normally the shaggers consisted of bat boys and ball boys, but in 1992 the Padres fielded a few more youngsters and, most importantly, a woman. Cheryl could play baseball. She had just graduated from Arizona State University on a softball scholarship and her abilities to field were fundamentally perfect. Cheryl was dressed like the others playing the outfield. She was told that in the beginning she should keep her ponytail under her cap.

After catching a couple of easy fly balls, she then caught a wicked line drive that was curving away from her. She made it look easy. The fans noticed her and when she let her pony tail out from her cap they realized that there was a girl playing in the outfield. The fans in the right-field stands started to cheer every time Cheryl caught a ball.

McGwire won the Derby that day but Cheryl stole the show!

1992 Cecil Fielder, Jose Canseco and God

There were a number of times in my life that I was blessed to be God's co-pilot.

In late January 1992, I accompanied "God," also known as National League umpire Doug Harvey, on a drive to Dodger Stadium.

Harvey is held in such awe by his fellow umps and players that some years ago they began calling him God. Initially, he recoiled at the appellation. He later dismissed it with a silent smile, wrote Jerome Holtzman for the *Chicago Tribune* in 1988.

Doug was selected to serve as home plate ump for a head-to-head home run derby between Jose Canseco and Cecil Fielder taped for a future show on Fox Sports.

During our drive north from San Diego on Interstate 5, with little to no prompting needed from me, Doug shared some of his incredible experiences from his Hall of Fame umpiring career.

Stories about Bob Gibson, Sandy Koufax, Willie Mays, Tom Lasorda, Lou Brock—enough to fill a book, which he did in 2014 (*They Called Me God: The Best Umpire Who Ever Lived*).

What a storyteller. Animated, colorful language, dramatic voice inflections and scrumptious, behind-the-scenes observations, opinions, and details. Needless to say I was riveted.

Since we were headed to Dodger Stadium, I asked Doug what memories he had of the ballpark. He quickly recalled his first game ever in the big leagues. It was the 1962 opener at Dodger Stadium. Not just the first game of the season but the Dodger Stadium opener, the first-ever official regular-season game at Chavez Ravine.

"When I stepped onto the field at Dodger Stadium, opening day, April 11, 1962, the size of the place and sold-out crowd amazed me," Doug recalled. "Remember, I was just a farm kid from the Imperial Valley. Between innings, Al Barlick, who had the plate that day, asked me, 'What do you think of this joint?'

"I told him, 'It looks like it could hold a lot of hay.'"

Thirty years later Doug pulled into a parking space close to a Dodger Stadium entrance. We stepped into the predominantly blue-hued Los Angeles baseball cathedral that was virtually empty.

I walked alongside Doug, noticing that his gait was with authoritative confidence but in a low-key manner all the while acutely aware of again being in familiar surroundings. When we reached the field, there were a dozen or so Fox TV producers, directors, cameramen along with gaffers, grips and best boys scurrying around.

Knowing that the day would be filled with photo ops, I brought my camera along, making sure to stay out of the way and snap some photos.

Oh, look over there. Isn't that Jim Palmer? It is. Click.

A young Price Fielder and father Cecil Fielder, with Doug Harvey in the
background.

I shot the set-up, the event and all the hangers-on.

For me, watching the home run contest unfold wasn't all
that exciting due to constant stopping and starting, changing

camera angles, adjusting microphones and impromptu production meetings.

I never saw the finished edit, but I'm sure it was condensed from the three-hour shoot to nine action-packed dramatic moments.

After a few hours, I was looking forward to the ride back to San Diego, hoping for bumper-to-bumper traffic to provide additional time for Doug to share with me more of his classic baseball stories.

I wasn't disappointed as there was heavy traffic, which meant more stories.

A week later, I looked through the photos I had printed. Among the shots, I caught Cecil Fielder and his stocky eight-year-old son, Prince. I recall overhearing Cecil say that his son was a great hitter, already able to hit a ball 300 feet or more.

Naturally, I didn't believe him at the time.

But I guess it's safe to say that Cecil's fatherly boast was no mere idle exaggeration, as Prince would have a 12-year major league career that produced 319 homers, very comparable to his dad's 13-year MLB career in which he also hit 319 round-trippers.

What a memorable day.

OMG.

1998 Mark McGwire

On September 8, 1998, like other nights after dinner, my wife and I decided to take our dog for a walk around our block. I wanted to get home quickly so I could watch the nationally televised baseball game between the St. Louis Cardinals and Chicago Cubs at Busch Stadium.

A couple of weeks earlier, as Mark McGwire approached Roger Maris's home run record, the Office of the Baseball Commissioner called me to see if I would reach out to the Maris family and determine their interest to be on hand when the new home-run record was about to be set. The Maris family—six adult children and Roger's wife Pat—was gracious, generous and classy. They agreed to attend what would be the record-breaking game.

By the time the Cardinals-Cubs game was about to start. I didn't want to miss it.

McGwire started that game with 61 homers, which tied Maris. Like everyone else, I knew that with three weeks left of the 1998 season it was merely a matter of time that my life-long hero's home-run record would be broken.

I didn't want McGwire to break the record but realized that records are made blah, blah, blah...broken.

Moments after McGwire's 62nd homer cleared the left-field fence down the line sailing just under the Konica sign, the local San Diego ABC-TV station called me at home, asking if they could come over to get my reaction for a taped interview that would be played on the news that evening. I agreed.

I was disappointed and sad that my childhood hero's home run record was eclipsed.

Sitting in my living room with the TV station video camera rolling, the sports reporter asked how I felt when Maris's record was broken.

Here's what I said: "My father was 14 years old when Babe Ruth hit his 60th home run in 1927. I was 13 years old when Maris hit his 61st home run, so I'm happy for all the 13- and 14-year-olds who were able to witness McGwire's 62nd homer."

I must confess after all these years, I lied. I wasn't happy then or when Aaron Judge hit his 62nd home run in 2022.

In my heart Roger Maris still held the single-season home run record at 61.

Chapter 8

Tonk

When Roger Maris hit 61 home runs to break Babe Ruth's home run record in 1961, I was an impressionable 13-year-old.

My appetite for information, photos and memorabilia about Maris was insatiable. I was consumed with anything and everything about him.

When I wasn't at school or watching or listening to Yankee games or playing baseball, I spent my days and nights obsessively scouring newspapers, searching for anecdotes, facts and tidbits about Maris.

One of my discoveries was sequestered in the July 4, 1961, sports section of the *Detroit Free Press*.

It was at this point during the 1961 season that Maris had knocked out 30 homers and was 11 games ahead of Ruth's fabled total of 60 back in 1927.

In anticipation of the upcoming Independence Day Yankee doubleheader in the Bronx against the Detroit Tigers, *Free Press* staff writer Bob Pille wrote an article about the Yankees and their penchant for hitting home runs.

The article's headline was, "Yanks Count on 'Tonks.'"

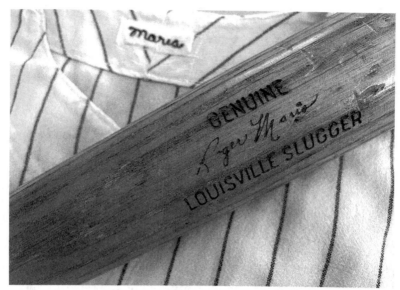

The sound of Roger Maris' Louisville Slugger bat hitting an American League Spaulding baseball squarely produces the sound of "tonk."

In his article, Pille noted that against the Washington Senators, the New Yorkers had hit five home runs on Sunday, July 2, with a final score of 13-4.

The Detroit sportswriter noted that most of the homers were of the "tonk" variety and explained that the word was the Yankees' own name for the big blasts.

Maris was quoted in the newspaper as saying, "You know when you hit a ball good, it goes 'tonk. 'Damned if I know how to spell it. It's just 'tonk.'"

Pille wrote, "The Yankees hit enough 'tonks' Sunday for one New York writer to call it 'the most raw power ever demonstrated in one game.'"

Just like a special decoder ring, I was hoping to be the only kid on the block who knew that "tonk" was the secret insider's name for home runs.

To impress my friends, my plan was to use my favorite new word only sparingly in conversation and with discretion, so as not to overdo it.

In the article, Pille provided detailed information about how far each of the five homers hit by Elston Howard, Mickey Mantle, Bill Skowron and two by Roger Maris had travelled.

With the Tigers about to face the Bronx Bombers, Pille concluded his story by quoting Tiger manager Bob Scheffing.

Asked his reaction to the Yankees' homers, Scheffing said, "I don't care how far they hit them, just how often."

On August 24, 1961 *Newsday* also referenced the word tonk by writing "Maris is Maris, a 197-pound athlete from Kansas City who loves to 'nosh' at a midtown delicatessen and 'tonk the ball' for long home runs."

On September 26, in his *Decatur Review* newspaper column "Sports in Review," Forrest R. Kyle wrote about Ty Cobb's new book and how he made a number of disparaging remarks about the hitting ability of the current major league heroes who swing for the fences.

To illustrate his point, Kyle wrote that New York sportswriter Leonard Shecter discussed the "home run epidemic" with Roger Maris, Mickey Mantle and Ralph Houk for an article he was writing for the November issue of *SPORT* magazine.

Kyle lifted a Maris quote from the article, "You can't make money beating out ground balls. I'll take that one tonk with men on base every time."

Then for clarification purposes Kyle informed his readers: A "tonk" is a home run.

Shecter's story was written well in advance of the magazine's November cover date because the only reference to the amount of home runs hit in 1961 was 40 by Maris. Therefore, the deadline for the article was prior to August 4 when Maris hit home run number 41.

Shecter further explained, "It's almost a sensual thing, this wallop of bat on baseball when it's "the big tonk."

Then, in response to the constant talk that the 1961 baseballs are different than the old days of baseball, Shecter quoted Maris, "I get sick and tired of hearing that. These old guys say the ball is juiced up because they were a bunch of 'Punch and Judy' hitters. Look at the way they held their bats. They'd hit .400 but it would take four hits to get a run. We get it with one tonk."

At 13 years old, *tonk* was all mine. I devoured it. I owned it. I treasured it.

It's my favorite baseball word, and always will be.

Chapter 9

Bounce HRs

One final thought about home runs.

As the 1961 baseball season progressed, newspapers across the country were filled with stories about Mickey Mantle and Roger Maris in pursuit of Babe Ruth's single-season record of 60 homers.

It was during that season when, at 13 years old, I first became aware of the fact that during Ruth's homer record in 1927, balls that bounced over the fence and into the stands went into the record books as home runs.

In fact, from 1889 until 1931, a batted ball that bounced in fair territory, at some minimum distance from home plate (gradually extended from 210 feet to 250 feet), and then into the stands or over, through or under a barrier, was considered a home run.

So, the question on every baseball fan's mind was this: Did Ruth ever hit a bounce home run during the 1927 season? Alas, as reported in multiple newspapers, the answer was (and is) no.

Furthermore, it was pointed out that none of Ruth's 714 career homers were of the bounce variety.

As for a ball bouncing into the stands or over, through or

under a barrier, the rule clarification was changed in 1931 with a simple addition subsection added to "Rule 41. Balls Batted Outside the Playing Field": "A fair hit ball that bounds into a stand or over a fence shall be a two-base hit," which I referred to then and now as a ground-rule double.

And which I found out is a misnomer. It should be called a "rule-book double" because ground rules vary from park to park and deal with unique elements related to each park.

So, the ball that bounces into the stands or over, through or under a barrier is consistently applied to all ballparks based on today's Rule 5.05, hence the appropriate name that to this day no one uses.

If Ruth didn't hit any "bounce home runs," were any of those that were hit attributed to any players of significance?

Yes!

The 1925 American League baseball was 9 to 9¼ inches in circumference with a weight of 5 to 5¼ oz.

Lou Gehrig, the Yankees' first baseman, ranks high as a player of note who was credited with two "bounce Home runs" during his Hall of Fame career. Both occurred at Yankee Stadium.

The first was a grand slam that Gehrig hit against the Washington Senators on July 23, 1925. It was the first of 23 grand slams he hit in his career.

The other Gehrig "bounce homer" was on July 30, 1927 versus the Cleveland Indians.

With more than a few drips of irony, both of the Iron Man's bounce homers undermine two significant baseball records:

- The first being that Gehrig held the record for most career grand slams (23) for more than 70 years, even though one of them was a bounce home run that

today would be incorrectly called a ground rule
double but ruled a "rule-book double."

- The all-time grand-slam homer record now belongs
  to Alex Rodriguez, who eclipsed that mark in 2013
  and had a total of 25 slams in his career.
- The other record impacted was most home runs hit in
  a season (1927) by two players on the same team
  (Ruth 60, and Gehrig 47). Those 107 homers stood as
  the record until Maris (61) and Mantle (54) eclipsed it
  in 1961 with a combined total of 115.

Thanks to SABR (Society for American Baseball Research) a
major league baseball Home Run Log is maintained which
contains substantial data on bounce home runs (BHRs), who hit
them, where and when, from 1876 through 1930.

Chart 1. Number of Bounce HRs (1901-1930)			
Seasons	Total Home Runs (MLB)	Bounce HRs	Bounce HRs as % of Total
1901-1910	3,207	178	5.6%
1911-1919	4,170	268	6.4%
1920	630	24	3.8%
1921	937	43	4.6%
1922	1,055	69	6.5%
1923	980	64	6.5%
1924	896	28	3.1%
1925	1,169	28	2.4%
1926	863	20	2.3%
1927	922	21	2.3%
1928	1,093	11	1.0%
1929	1,349	33	2.4%
1930	1,565	20	1.3%
1920-1930	11,459	361	3.2%
Total 1901-30	18,836	807	4.3%

All charts by Ron Selter.

From 1901 through 1930, of the nearly 19,000 home runs

that were hit, 807 BHRs were recorded, which represented 4.3 percent of the total. Chart 1 shows the number of BHRs through the 30-year period. The 19-year period of 1901-1919 is considered the Deadball Era of baseball, while the 1920s ushered in an era, led by Babe Ruth, where home runs take on a larger role and increased in numbers. The number of BHRs spiked in 1922-23 at 6.5 percent of the total home runs hit.

In the last year that BHRs were allowed, 1930, the ratio of BHRs had dropped to 1.3 percent. Some of this reduction reflected the American League ballparks changing their ground rules for the 1930 season to prohibit BHRs.

The four players with the most BHRs are shown in Chart 2.

Chart 2. Players With Most Bounce HRs (1901-1930)					
	Career				Period When His Bounce HRs Hit
Player	Bounce HRs	Total HR	% Bounce HRs	Team(s)	
Gavy Cravath	10	119	8.4%	Philadelphia (NL)	1913-1919
Fred Luderus	9	84	10.7%	Philadelphia (NL)	1912-1916
Dode Paskert	8	42	19.0%	Cincinnati (1) Philadelphia (NL) (6) Chicago (NL) (1)	1908-1918
Johnny Mokan	8	32	25.0%	Philadelphia (NL)	1922-1925

Topping the list was Gavy Cravath, who played for the Philadelphia Phillies at the time. In fact, three of the top four BHR hitters played for the Phillies. Cravath's 10 BHRs were all hit during the Deadball Era.

He was one of major-league baseball's first recognized home run hitters, and in the decade 1911-1920, he hit 117 home runs, the most in baseball. Cravath led the major leagues in home runs in four separate seasons: 1913, 1914, 1915, and 1917

Chart 3. Bounce HRs of Noted Hall of Famers				
Player	Bounce HRs	Total HR	Career % BHR of Total HR	Years Played
Home Run Baker	3	96	3.1%	1908-1922
Ty Cobb	3	117	2.6%	1905-1928
Lou Gehrig	2	493	0.4%	1923-1939
Rogers Hornsby	2	301	0.7%	1915-1937
Tris Speaker	5	117	4.3%	1907-1928
Casey Stengel	5	60	8.3%	1912-1925
Honus Wagner	3	101	3.0%	1897-1917
Hack Wilson	4	244	1.6%	1923-1934

Listed in Chart 3 are a number of Hall of Fame players who had BHRs. Outfielder Casey Stengel, had five BHRs, or 8.3 percent of his career home runs came after a bounce.

In summary, all of this confirms the idiom that sometimes in life, but more often in baseball, that's the way the ball bounces.

A Chat with Arthur Hano

My favorite nonfiction baseball book is *A Day in The Bleachers* by Arnold Hano.

The book not only captures the onfield action of Game 1 of the 1954 World Series, but it also places the reader directly in the ballpark as a result of Hano sitting in the Polo Ground bleachers for that game.

Arnold's prose appeared often in *SPORT* Magazine, my publication of choice while growing up in the 1950s and '60s.

A perfect example of Hano's writing genius would be his description of the line drive Willie McCovey of the San Francisco Giants hit to the Yankees' Bobby Richardson, ending the 1962 World Series.

Hano wrote, "A scream of rising joy had been strangled."

A few sentences later, Hano described the difference between the almost-identical final-game statistics of the winning pitcher, Ralph Terry, and the losing pitcher, Jack Sanford, writing: "You cannot slip a woman's silken hair between them, that is how similar they are."

A writer of Hano's talent comes along but once in a hundred years.

Book launch party of *A Day In the Bleachers* by Arnold Hano in a special handmade edition with illustrations by Mark Ulriksen. (Liz Hafalia/San Francisco Chronicle via AP)

Arnold was an astute baseball fan who began attending baseball games at the age of four in 1926. His lifetime baseball experiences included watching thousands of ballgames and reporting conversations with hundreds of players ranging from Babe Ruth to Dave Kingman.

Hano was the logical choice to talk about home runs as he was an astute observer of baseball for almost 100 years.

When I called him with my request, he laughed and apologetically said, "I'm 99 years old and legally blind, but I want to help you. Let's have a conversation over the phone and you can ask me anything you want."

Here is our July 1, 2021 phone conversation that I purposely formatted similar to *SPORT* Magazine's "Sound Off" interview series of the 1960s.

~

Strasberg: What memories do you have of attending your first Major League Baseball game?

Hano: It was at the Polo Grounds when I was 4 years old in 1926. I went with my father and we sat between home and first base.

Strasberg: Did you take the subway?

Hano: I got there by falling out of bed because I was living one block from the Polo Grounds.

Strasberg: What do you recall about that game?

Hano: How wide Giants first basemen Bill Terry played away from first base. I thought a first baseman played near first base. But he was out in short right field, practically, and I couldn't understand it. Then, as soon as the ball was hit to the infielder, he was there at first base. He would float over there as quickly as possible.

Strasberg: What's your earliest recollection of Babe Ruth?

Hano: I probably was aware of Babe Ruth during that same 1926 season.

Strasberg: Did you ever see Babe Ruth hit a home run? If so, can you describe it?

Hano: He hit a ball that looked as though it went straight up. He hit towering home runs and the ball would come down somewhere in the right-field seats. But it always had a towering quality about it. T-O-W-E-R-I-N-G, towering.

Strasberg: Did you sense an anticipation from the crowd that he would hit a home run when he got up to bat?

Hano: I felt the anticipation because I was part of it. I began as a Yankee fan, not as a Giant fan. I began as a Yankee fan because of Babe Ruth, and when he got up, I thought, "Oh, he's going to hit a home run. He will hit a home run every time I see him get up."

I remember that the kids around me were very excited about Babe Ruth, and the chatter of kids would increase quickly when he came to the plate.

Strasberg: How old were you when you were allowed to go to ballgames without an adult chaperone?

Hano: Almost immediately after my first game.

We lived one block from the Polo Grounds. My grandfather was a high-ranking police officer and he had passes to both Yankee Stadium and the Polo Grounds. I don't recall whether we had Ebbets Field passes.

To get to the Polo Grounds, I would cross one street, which I learned to cross when I was 4 years old. My grandfather would be outside the ballpark, and he'd see me and take me to the box office. Something happened at the box office, and I was let into the ballpark by myself.

When the game was over, I would let the crowd sort of disappear. I'd wait there until I could retreat across that same street and be home. I lived in a house on Edgecombe Avenue, the same house that the Meusel brothers, Bob of the Yankees and his brother "Irish" of the Giants, lived in. They lived either one floor above me or below me, so when one was home playing ball the other was on the road playing ball.

When I went by myself, I think my passes put me somewhere between home and first. At a certain point, I got a little bored by it and it seemed to me there was more excitement out in the bleachers. I don't know when I started going to the bleachers, but it was pretty early on. Maybe I was 7 or 8.

Strasberg: Is it fair to say that your baseball upbringing was as a bleacherite?

Hano: I love being in the bleachers. One of the first dates I ever had was with Marian Rose, a girl on my street. I would've been 12 years old and said to her, "I'd like to go to the ballgame tomorrow. Would you like to go with me?" She said, "Sure."

I bought two bleacher seats. When we went up the ramp and arrived at the seats, she looked around, grabbed my arm and said, "No women?" That had not occurred to me.

Strasberg: Oh, wow.

Hano: She was right. There were only guys sitting around. I shrugged and that was that. I remember distinctly in that ballgame, Travis Jackson hit a fly ball along the left-field line that grazed the seats as it came down. Somebody sitting near us yelled, "Chinese home run, Travis." Marian said to me, "What does that mean?" I said, "Well, he didn't really blast it."

She got up out of her seat and ran to the lip of the bleachers and yelled, "Attaboy, Travis." She came back a fully fledged bleacherite. Things like that stuck with me.

Strasberg: Do you have a favorite Ruth game memory?

Hano: In 1933, my father came into our kitchen, where my brother and I were doing the dishes, he said, "Boys, let's go to Yankee Stadium tomorrow, the Babe's going to pitch."

The Washington Senators had clinched the pennant and the Yankees were, I think, seven games out, and so the Yankees, just to be smart about getting some folks into the ballpark, announced that Babe Ruth would pitch the ballgame against the Red Sox on the last day of the '33 season.

I said to my brother, who was three years older than me, "Do you think he's going to pitch the whole ballgame?" I thought maybe he'd just show up, pitch an inning or two and that's it.

My brother said, "No, if they announced he's going to pitch, if he goes OK, he'll pitch OK," and he pitched the entire game.

He gave up 12 hits, the Yankees beat the Red Sox 6-5. Besides pitching, Babe hit his 34th home run of the season in that game.

Strasberg: Did you ever meet Ruth?

Hano: Well, two days after that game, I was on 80th Street and Broadway, and here came a larger-than-life Babe Ruth crossing the street with his wife and his daughter, wearing his signature camelhair long top coat sweeping down the sidewalk and so I ran across the street.

Traffic stopped, I ran up to him and said, "Babe, I saw you pitch that game a couple of days ago." He looked at me and ruffled my hair and said, "Yeah, kid." I said, "How come you didn't strike out anybody?"

He'd given up 12 hits, and he didn't strike out anybody. He answered, "I want those seven palookas behind me to earn their keep." His wife rolled her eyes, and he laughed and I laughed.

That was the end of my conversation with Babe Ruth when I was 11 years old.

Strasberg: You grew up in the beginning of the evolution of how home runs overtook the game of baseball. Was that disappointing to you?

Hano: No, I don't recall that I was disappointed. To me, as it became a home-run hitter's game, it became my game. I just absorbed them, expected them, appreciated them.

In fact, I remember playing in the backyard where I kept thinking, "Gee, I'm going to hit a home run, I'm going to hit a home run." That sort of feeling went through me.

Strasberg: The year that you were born Ken Williams of the St. Louis Browns hit over 30 home runs. Any thoughts about him?

Hano: I don't think about him. At least my mind doesn't operate like that. You are taking advantage of somebody at 99 whose mind just leaks.

(*Pause*)

When I walk, I leave a trail of pronouns behind me.

Strasberg: After you became a sportswriter you had an opportunity to interview many players. I'll mention a few noted home-run hitters, hoping you'll provide some insight.

Willie Mays.

Hano: Willie Mays. Yes. I had conversations with Willie when he first broke in. I talked to him because he seemed very willing and wanting to be part of the action around him. That was the case from the time he played stickball in the street, which I also did, into him breaking in as a hot-shot young ballplayer.

I remember the *SPORT* Magazine editor Al Silverman said to me, "Do a piece about the loneliness of a young ballplayer." I suggested the story to Mays, he said, "What will they pay me?" He had learned that he was a commodity and I said, "Gee, I don't know. I don't think anything."

Willie said, "Well, then forget it. Because I could tell you a lot about that experience if they would pay me." I reported back to Silverman, and he said, "No, we don't pay for these things." I went back to Willie and told him, he said, "Well, that's too bad then."

Strasberg: Eventually you did write a book about Mays.

Hano: Oh, yes, I did a book about Mays. The people who put out *SPORT* asked me to do it.

It was one of those unauthorized biographies. The book sold 480,000 copies, which was more than all the other books about Willie Mays put together.

Strasberg: Did you interview Mays for that book?

Hano: I would see him after games and things like that, but I never told him I was doing the book. I just did it with the feeling of, "Gee, this isn't the right thing to do, but this is the way they want me to do it, so that's the way I'll do it."

Strasberg: After the book came out, what did Willie think of it?

Hano: After he saw that it was a popular book and that people were talking about it, he started to become very cold toward me. He realized I was the person who had this power to write about him whether he liked it or not and didn't pay him.

He started saying to me, "Get off my back. We've had enough of this."

Strasberg: Any Dick Stuart stories?

Hano: I did a piece on Stuart when he got traded after the 1962 season from the Pirates to the Red Sox. He was so full of himself. It was astonishing. He really believed that people would say, "There goes Dick Stuart, the greatest batter that ever lived."

He thought of himself in that way, and he thought anything I could do to elevate him or to help him to be accepted as "the greatest ballplayer ever" would make him happy.

Strasberg: How about your experiences with Roberto Clemente?

Hano: Well, Roberto Clemente was very different. I was sympathetic to the plight of Latin ballplayers. I saw immediately that Clemente was a great natural ballplayer who was treated subserviently. The Pittsburgh press was terrible. Everything about how they treated him was bad.

Myron Cope did that 1966 *Sports Illustrated* article about him being baseball's champion hypochondriac. The illustration for the article had a drawing of Clemente's body with different ailments next to his head for headaches, bone chips in his right elbow, a stomach disorder, injured tendon, etc.

Cope didn't understand that for Latin players when someone greeted them by saying, "How are you?" instead of saying "I'm fine," they would tell you because they thought you were interested in how they were.

As a result of that misunderstanding, they were considered whiners, crybabies and things like that. He was treated maliciously and badly by people who should've known better.

Strasberg: So you got along with Clemente?

Hano: He liked me enormously as a result of me being sympathetic to his situation. I had his phone number and could phone him in the middle of the night to talk to him about whatever when he was down in Puerto Rico. He enjoyed my intervening into his life because he knew he was going to be treated fairly.

Strasberg: You had a special friendship with Stan Musial of the St. Louis Cardinals, who hit 475 career homers. Did you talk hitting?

Hano: One time, I said to him the day before the 1946 World Series, "You're going to be facing pitchers that you've never seen before. Even with all the scouting reports, that's going to be new to you."

I said, "What do you do? Do you go there expecting a fastball and adjust to the curve?" "No, no, no," he said, "I always know what the pitcher is throwing, whether it's going to be a fastball or curve, I know that."

Then I said, "What do you do, you steal signs?" He said, "No, no, no, I can tell when the ball comes out of the pitcher's hand. Five feet out of the pitcher's hand, I can tell by the rotation."

This was one of my first experiences with the incredible quality that hitters have, their ability to see so much better than the rest of us. He could tell by the rotation what the pitch was only five feet after the pitcher had thrown the ball.

That year, it didn't seem to matter because he ended up hitting .222 in that World Series.

Another thing was on his last game of his career in 1963, I remember sitting idly in a car with him and people would see him in the car and shout to him. They treated him like a brother, and he would shout back to them, wave his hand, and he would laugh.

When Stan laughed, he giggled. He had a girlish giggle. I remember that.

In the locker room, he was holding up his uniform so you could see his number. He had it right side up then upside down so his number was 6 or 9 and said, "Now, I'm me. Now I'm Ted Williams. Now I'm me."

Some reporter said to him, "I saw your first game in 1941. You had two hits in that first game, and you had two hits in this your last game. You haven't improved a bit," which made him giggle.

That's just the way he was. He very much enjoyed public acclaim. The press treated him beautifully. On occasion he would smoke a cigar, but they never took a picture of him smoking.

Strasberg: Mickey Mantle and Roger Maris. Do you recall the home run race during the 1961 season?

Hano: I attended many of those Yankee games because I remember rooting against Maris because I was rooting for Babe Ruth. I don't recall that I pitted Maris versus Mantle, but I was pitting each of them, particularly Maris, against Babe Ruth.

Strasberg: Did you sense that your contemporaries felt the same way?

Hano: I think so. A lot of people were prejudiced against Maris because of their innate attraction and love of Babe Ruth. To me, Ruth and his records seemed sacrosanct. I didn't want to see anybody touching it.

Strasberg: What was the talk among sportswriters in 1961 regarding the single-season home run record?

Hano: I'm guessing at this, but I think most of them felt that no one was going to hit more than 60. They thought it was going to be an interesting fight, but that nobody would hit more than 60. I couldn't tell whether that pleased them or displeased them.

Strasberg: Which side of the fence were you on regarding the new extended schedule that season?

Hano: It bothered me that the 1961 schedule had 8 more games than Ruth's 1927 schedule. You know what I mean? The 154- to 162-game season. That's a record where I almost wanted it to have an asterisk.

Then when I read Jane Leavy's book *The Big Fella* about Babe Ruth, I discovered how many times Ruth had been taken out by the seventh inning for defensive purposes. Therefore, he missed opportunities in the seventh, eighth and ninth innings to hit another home run.

I became aware of that, but I still felt that Maris was playing more games than Ruth played and therefore it shouldn't count. I didn't think it shouldn't count. I knew it should count, but I was a Babe Ruth fan, not a Yankee fan. But with Maris, you had to be a Yankee fan and that was not me.

Strasberg: Did you know Dave Kingman?

Hano: I had lots of conversations with Dave Kingman, starting in 1971 when he was a rookie with the Giants.

Too much was being expected of him. Did you know that Kingman had four home runs, two doubles and a triple before he hit his first major-league single? Then in 1972 his manager Charlie Fox experimented to make him a 6-6 third baseman, a position he had never played before in his life.

Naturally, it didn't work. Even after Kingman had been in the big leagues for a while, too much was expected of him.

Strasberg: Throughout your life, there have been many memorable home runs. What comes to mind when you think about Bobby Thomson's dramatic playoff home run in 1951 for the New York Giants against the Brooklyn Dodgers?

Hano: I was working then for a publishing house [Lion Books], and I remember listening on the radio to that ninth inning. Larry Graver, who worked in the art department, was a Dodger fan.

He was walking with a piece of paper in his hand just as Russ Hodges went into his call, "The Giants win the pennant! The Giants win the pennant!" Graver turned white. He blanched. He lost his step, and then continued walking.

I loved that moment, I just loved it. I think it was Willie Mays who shouted at Thomson near home plate, "Touch the plate, touch the plate, touch the plate."

Strasberg: Do you recall Bill Mazeroski's 1960 World Series home run?

Hano: I remember right after the game Danny Murtaugh said, "If my wife wants to know who I would kiss first, no matter what she thinks, I'd kiss Bill Mazeroski."

Strasberg: How about Barry Bonds and his 73rd home run?

Hano: I didn't care about it. I thought early on that the guy was a fraud. He had a great swing, and he was a wonderful athlete and all that, but he was playing on juice of some sort. That's how I felt.

Strasberg: So, who do you think is the lifetime career home run hitter?

Hano: I keep thinking it's Babe Ruth. No matter what you tell me, it's Babe Ruth.

Strasberg: Arnold, I want to express my deepest gratitude for answering my questions and sharing your stories. Thank you, thank you, thank you.

Hano: Listen, you're more than welcome. Thank you. It's been my pleasure.

~

Sadly, Arnold Hano never reached his desired goal of 100 years old. Two days before the 2021 World Series he passed away on October 24, 2021, but his masterful writing lives on for all of us to enjoy.

Acknowledgments

This is my opportunity to extend my appreciation to those wonderful people who assisted me with this project.

First, let me respectfully acknowledge my wife, Patti, who played a significant role in allowing me to spend an inordinate amount of time researching, writing and compiling the chapters for this book.

Due to my extremely good fortune, I proudly acknowledge my ongoing friendship with the Roger Maris family that began with Roger himself outside Yankee Stadium in 1962 and then in 1968 when I first met his wife, Pat.

Later, I met the next generation of the Maris family in 1985 when I was introduced to their children: Susan, Roger Jr., Sandra, Kevin, Richard, and Randy and eventually their spouses and children.

Also, I could not overstate the investment of time and talent that John Freeman and Dave Wright provided. They lent their sharp writing and editing skills when I often needed wording enhanced, sentences reconstructed, and paragraphs moved around and gently edited so there was more continuity and clarity in my writing.

Very much appreciated for this endeavor is the artistry of Rich Kee and Todd Radom.

Great thanks, as well, to Marty Appel, who never hesitated to provide guidance whenever I needed it.

Then there's my foundation of ongoing dear friendships that I have enjoyed, in some cases, dating back 60 years.

Those include: Peter and Joyce Briante, Arnie and Debra Cardillo, Cheryl Smith Lemox, Jim Gold, Jim and Janice Healy, Duane Dimock, Susan Mendolia, Doug and Joy Harvey, Tom Larwin, Tim Wiles, Bret Moutaw, Dave Greene, Lloyd Kuritsky, Kevin Baskin, Peter Stolpe, R. C. Stolpe, Mike and Jeanette McDuffee, Phil Cuzzi, Amanda Hamels, Belinda Bird, Jeff and Li-An Merideth, Pete Miesner, Dick and Susan Dent, Howard Frank, Tom Shieber, Scott Keene, Roger and Mary Bow, Greg Howell, Leslie Hansen, Ron Seaver, Rena Bell, Dick Freeman, Ballard Smith, David Kramer, Brian Richards,, Kirk Kenney, Mr. Clements, Ray Simons, Randy Wooden, Bob Costas, Mark Chiarello, Rob Johnson, Ted Leitner, Pat Gallagher, Jon Leonoudakis and my adorable niece Julie, her children Jefferson and Sydney and her husband Vincent Belardino.

Photographically, I'm indebted to photographers Frank B. Jones Sr., Don Sturkey, Larry Carpa and Fred O. Rodgers. I very much appreciated the assistance of Sarah Carrier of the North Carolina Collection Photographic Archives, Wilson Special Collections Library, University of North Carolina at Chapel Hill; Lauren Menges of the Durham County Library; Shana Hoover of Restoration Newsmedia; Danielle Prichett of the Greensboro Public Library Central Branch; Tammy L. Medlin of the Wilson County Public Library North Carolina and Molly

G. Rawls of Forsyth County Public Library Photographic Collection, Winston-Salem, North Carolina.

And a tip of the cap to Johnny Smith, Charlie Hertlein, Bob Godfrey, Jack McKeon, Jim Gentile, Duane Kuiper and Arnold Hano who in 2021 agreed to share their memories.

About the Author

Andy Strasberg is the author of the best-selling *My 1961*, also from August Publications. His working in and writing about the profession of baseball includes 22 years in marketing with the San Diego Padres and 18 years representing high-profile players, as well as consulting for Major League Baseball teams and the National Baseball Hall of Fame in Cooperstown, N.Y.

He was a contributor to Ken Burns' award-winning PBS documentary *Baseball*, consulted for Billy Crystal's HBO movie *61**, staged a baseball exhibit at the Lincoln Center for the Performing Arts, proposed and consulted on the 2008 U.S. Postal Service commemorative stamp for the game's anthem, "Take Me Out to the Ball Game," and negotiated key sponsorships for the National Baseball Hall of Fame.